MARCO  POLO

CALI FOR NIA

CANADA

Washington
Oregon
California
Sacramento
San Francisco
Los Angeles
Nevada
Idaho
Montana
Wyoming
Utah
Denver
Colorado
Arizona
New Mexico
North Dakota
South Dakota
Nebraska
Iowa
USA
Kansas
Oklahoma
Texas

MEXICO

www.marco-polo.com

FREE!

THE TOURING APP

shows you the way...
including routes and offline maps!

2

GET MORE OUT OF YOUR MARCO POLO GUIDE

IT'S AS SIMPLE AS THIS

1 go.marco-polo.com/cal

2 download and discover

GO!

WORKS OFFLINE!

6 **INSIDER TIPS**
Our top 15 Insider Tips

8 **BEST OF ...**
- ⬤ Great places for free
- ⬤ Only in California
- ⬤ And if it rains?
- ⬤ Relax and chill out

12 **INTRODUCTION**
Discover California!

18 **WHAT'S HOT**
There are lots of new things
to discover in California

20 **IN A NUTSHELL**
Background information
on California

26 **FOOD & DRINK**
Top culinary tips

30 **SHOPPING**
For a fun-filled
shopping spree!

32 **SAN FRANCISCO**

44 **THE NORTH**
44 Eureka/Northern Coast
48 Lassen Volcanic 49 Mendocino 50 Mount Shasta 54 Napa
Valley 53 Sonoma Valley

56 **CENTRAL CALIFORNIA**
58 Gold Country 60 Highway
1/Big Sur 62 Monterey Peninsula 63 Lake Tahoe 64 Sac-

ramento 66 San Luis Obispo
68 Santa Barbara 70 Sequoia/
Kings Canyon 71 Yosemite

SYMBOLS

INSIDER TIP	Insider Tip
★	Highlight
⬤⬤⬤⬤	Best of ...
⍭	Scenic view
◍	Responsible travel: for fair trade and ecology aspects
(*)	Telephone numbers that are not toll-free

PRICE CATEGORIES HOTELS

Expensive	over $230
Moderate	$130–230
Budget	under $130

Prices are for a double room
per night without breakfast

PRICE CATEGORIES RESTAURANTS

Expensive	over $40
Moderate	$25–40
Budget	under $25

Prices are for a main course
with soup/salad in the evening, lunchtime prices are
usually significantly lower

CONTENTS

74 LOS ANGELES

86 THE SOUTH
87 Anaheim 89 Colorado River Area 90 Death Valley 92 Laguna Beach 93 Palm Springs 95 San Diego

100 DISCOVERY TOURS
100 California at a glance
104 A paradise for adventure seekers: the untamed north

107 Surf's up, sun's out: the hot south and its deserts
109 Into the desert: Las Vegas and Death Valley

112 SPORTS & ACTIVITIES
Activities for all seasons

116 TRAVEL WITH KIDS
Best things to do with kids

120 FESTIVALS & EVENTS
All dates at a glance

122 LINKS, BLOGS, APPS & MORE
Plan ahead and use on the go

124 TRAVEL TIPS
From A to Z

130 ROAD ATLAS

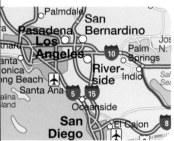

142 INDEX & CREDITS

144 DOS & DON'TS

DID YOU KNOW?
Timeline → p. 14
Patent 139.121 → p. 24
Local specialities → p. 28
Wooden records → p. 73
Stage-set city L.A. → p. 81
Threat of the desert → p. 91
Public holidays → p. 121
Currency converter → p. 125
For bookworms and film buffs → p. 126
Budgeting → p. 127
Weather → p. 128

MAPS IN THE GUIDEBOOK
(132 A1) Page numbers and co-ordinates refer to the road atlas
(138/139 A1) Map of Los Angeles
(U A1) Coordinates for the map of San Francisco inside the back cover
Coordinates are also given for places not marked on the road atlas

(🛇 A–B 2–3) refers to the removable pull-out map
(🛇 a–b 2–3) refers to the map of San Francisco on the pull-out map

INSIDE FRONT COVER:
The best Highlights

INSIDE BACK COVER:
Map of San Francisco

The best MARCO POLO Insider Tips

Our top 15 Insider Tips

INSIDER TIP Views from a steep slope
At *Glacier Point* you're standing nearly 1,000 m/3,280 ft above the valley bottom of Yosemite National Park (photo above). Many visitors shy away from the long drive in, but it's well worth it → **p. 71**

INSIDER TIP The desert is alive!
See kangaroo rats and snakes in the cactus gardens of the *Living Desert*, Palm Springs. In the late afternoon the animals become active → **p. 94**

INSIDER TIP The wildest rollercoasters
In *Knott's Berry Farm* near Anaheim it's a long way down, in freefall. The lights of big neighbour Disney might shine a little brighter, but these rides are well worth a try → **p. 89**

INSIDER TIP Fancy some tacos?
The stalls at Los Angeles' vibrant *Grand Central Market* serve the best Mexican snacks – and you'll probably be the only gringos here → **p. 77**

INSIDER TIP Pure America
Traditional – and very American: fairs such as the *San Diego County Fair* (photo right) seem so retro that they appear stuck in the 1960s. Fabulously kitsch, and often there's a parade thrown in as well → **p. 120**

INSIDER TIP A latte with a view
The Saturday morning *farmer's market* of Northern California's organic producers at San Francisco's Ferry Building is a popular meeting point. The shores of the Bay offer pretty views of the Oakland Bay Bridge → **p. 40**

INSIDER TIP Deep in the "Red Man's Country"
With flashy signs and huge figures, the *Trees of Mystery* attraction in Redwood National Park seems like a tourist trap. But the small, rather old-fashioned *museum* dedicated to the history of the "First Americans" is definitely worth a visit – and it doesn't cost a cent → **p. 47**

INSIDER TIP Stroll on the Plaza

In *Sonoma*, folk meet on the municipal square, which oozes pioneer-era charm → **p. 54**

INSIDER TIP Welcome to the wine tasting

The *Edna Valley* near San Luis Obispo might just be the new Napa Valley – the wines from the relatively unknown local wineries are excellent → **p. 67**

INSIDER TIP Avant-garde art

Bergamot Station in Santa Monica: a fun mixture of eccentric trendy shops, cafés and Californian art, a bit off the beaten tourist track → **p. 76**

INSIDER TIP Stargazing

They might be a few years away from stardom still, so for the time being young hopefuls are still waiting tables at the retro-eccentric *Mel's Drive-In* eatery on Sunset Boulevard in LA or propping up the bar → **p. 82**

INSIDER TIP Sheer adrenaline

With a *tandem flight*, even non-flyers can float in the air above Santa Barbara and enjoy vistas that very few visitors to California get to see → **p. 115**

INSIDER TIP Canter through the dunes

Can there be anything more beautiful than riding out on the beach on a clear morning? The Salinas River State Park near Monterey provides a magnificent backdrop → **p. 114**

INSIDER TIP Love and Peace

Explore *Haight-Ashbury* in San Francisco in the footsteps of the flower children, listening to fascinating stories about Janis Joplin and the Grateful Dead → **p. 39**

INSIDER TIP Steaks on the highway

The *AJ Spurs steakhouse* in Buellton serves up western flair and the best steaks only 100 yards from the US 101 heading to Santa Barbara → **p. 69**

BEST OF ...

GREAT PLACES FOR FREE
Discover new places and save money

● *Giant wheels in the Cable Car Museum*
While a trip on the rattling cable cars (photo) in San Francisco is not cheap, the *Cable Car Museum*, a squeaking, hissing and spitting relic of the industrial age where massive wheels power the miles-long cables, is free – and impressive → p. 35, 117

● *Be on TV – for free*
The star roles might be taken, but in Hollywood you can get on TV as a spectator without too much hard work. TV studios are always looking for claqueurs for game shows and so on. Who knows, a few years later that very series might appear on a network at home → p. 78

● *Victorian delights*
A locality like *Ferndale* really should charge to get in, it's that cute. They don't however, so feel free to enjoy the Victorian architecture built by the lumber barons for free → p. 46

● *Art for free – in Los Angeles*
The spectacular architecture and the works on display in the best art museum in California are indeed available free of charge – all thanks to Mr. Getty. The billionaire founder of the *Getty Museum* wanted to give everybody access to art. Equally stunning: the panoramic view across L.A. → p. 78

● *Free trip into the Wild West*
Camera at the ready? *Highway 49* snakes through the most authentic gold-rush western towns of Gold Country. In Jamestown or Columbia it feels like stepping back straight into the time of the pioneers – if it wasn't for the souvenir shops → p. 58

● *Gaudy show*
The traditional Pride Days of the gay and lesbian community are an experience, with the fabulously imaginative costumes fit for any stage – all without paying a penny. The most atmospheric parades are the ones in late June in San Francisco and West Hollywood → p. 120

●●●● Dots in guidebook refer to "Best of..." tips

● *Pedal across the Golden Gate*
Only by taking a tour by bike (or on foot) across the *Golden Gate Bridge* will you truly perceive the dimensions of this famous structure. The roadway lies over 80 m/262.5 ft above the Sound, and there's a howling wind. Still a great experience! → **p. 37**

● *Powder and Brylcream*
How is it that actors always look so good on camera? The Hollywood Museum allows you deep insights into the work of makeup artists – and the life of famous stars → **p. 79**

● *Holy Mountain*
You won't get more esoteric in California than this: Mount Shasta is a meeting point for ashram followers, interstellar visitors and philosophers of nature. If you're not interested in the extraterrestrials that are supposed to land at the foot of the snow-covered volcano (photo), just bag the summit → **p. 50**

● *Sightsea-ing on Highway 1*
Many reckon California's coast to be the world's most beautiful. We bet you'll agree if you drive on *Highway 1* around the cliffs of Big Sur. Every bend reveals a new panoramic view, another dramatic slope, another rock-rimmed beach → **p. 60**

● *The mother of all aquariums*
Head for the Californian underwater world: in the *Monterey Bay Aquarium* you'll find yourself at eye level with sharks, deep-sea creatures and glow-in-the dark jellyfish. Also: a three-storey forest of sea kelp! → **p. 63**

● *Valley of Death*
Over 50 °C/122 °F in the shade, 90 °C/194 °F in the sun are par for the course in the deepest part of *Death Valley*. The shimmering salt desert of Badwater lies nearly 100 m/328 ft below sea level and guarantees an experience of nature that's hot, hot, hot → **p. 90**

● *The perfect wave*
Tanned girls and athletic beach boys, a colourful scene in brewery pubs and cafés: *Huntington Beach* forms the pierced navel of the Californian surfing scene. The waves roll in evenly – just perfect for a practice class → **p. 93, 115**

ONLY IN

BEST OF ...

● *Singing in the rain...forest*
Drizzly weather in San Francisco? Why not roam the rainforest of the California Academy of Sciences: aquarium, planetarium, tropical hothouse and natural history show all rolled into one – and the icon of green technology in California → p. 35

● *Classy vintages*
You don't need the sun to go wine tasting in the Sonoma or Napa Valley. The Oxbow Public Market in Napa offers an alternative fare of oysters, cheese and wine paraphernalia → p. 53

● *Take the gold-rush train*
What would the Wild West have been without the railway? The huge California State Railroad Museum in Sacramento houses the most beautiful old locomotives and the luxury carriages of rich gold prospectors. All nicely protected from the elements → p. 65

● *Time travel into the virgin redwood forest*
Like a stage set from "Lord of the Rings": the giant trees in the Prairie Creek Redwoods State Park (photo). Patches of fog float between the massive trunks, drips fall from lush green branches. A waterproof jacket is all you need to dive into this untouched world full of secrets → p. 47

● *In the belly of an aircraft carrier*
There are not many chances in life to visit an aircraft carrier, right? In San Diego harbour the USS Midway invites you to all-weather tours through the imposing ship → p. 96

● *Dive down into the kelp forests*
Underwater rain or no rain – it doesn't matter. Let Truth Aquatics take you on a diving tour lasting one or several days in the spectacular kelp forests of the *Channel Islands National Park* off the coast at Santa Barbara. When you resurface, most likely the sun will be shining again → p. 69

RAIN

RELAX AND CHILL OUT
Take it easy and spoil yourself

● *Listen to the sea*
Unless there happens to be a wedding going on, enjoy wonderfully solitary and tranquil hours on the cliffs of *Patrick's Point State Park*. It won't be all quiet though – not with the Pacific crashing onto the wildly jagged rocks → **p. 48**

● *Wellness with volcanic ash*
Fancy a mudbath in volcanic ash and peat? The *Indian Springs Resort & Spa* in the small town of Calistoga at the northern end of Napa Valley offers traditional spa treatments. And there's lots more on offer in California's spas → **p. 53, 115**

● *Gone with the wind*
In *Bodie*, Sierra Nevada's most photogenic abandoned town, the ghosts of the Wild West still seem really close by. Sit down somewhere in a corner of this forsaken place, close your eyes and listen to the desert wind → **p. 73**

● *Alpine meadow idyll in Yosemite Park*
You can't get much higher up in California: the flowering mountain meadows below the *Tioga Pass* in Yosemite National Park are ideal for a picnic and a postprandial nap in the sun → **p. 71**

● *Boardwalk in Venice Beach*
Make yourself comfortable on one of the benches on Ocean Front Walk in *Venice Beach*, and let the outlandish parade of Angelenos pass by as if on an open air stage. If there is one place where California showcases its entire universe of creative weirdness, it's Venice Beach at weekends (photo) → **p. 80**

● *Relax on the rocks*
Aromatic sage, sun-warmed granite rocks, the call of the falcon in the distance: few experiences are more relaxing than sitting in the late afternoon somewhere in the rocky maze of the *Joshua Tree National Park* near Palm Springs → **p. 95**

INTRODUCTION

DISCOVER CALIFORNIA!

California is the dream destination on the Pacific, America's most enticing blend of stunning nature, cool cities and friendly eccentric people. After the legendary trek to the West, the pioneers discovered their promised land in this region. Despite great hardships, for many the American Dream turned reality here. To this day, the stretch of land between the Sierra Nevada and the Pacific has lost none of its fascination.

In contrast to those days, today the landscape may be explored and enjoyed in comfort by car. The Golden State is the ideal *destination for individualists* who want to experience nature at their own pace without having to forego the amenities of civilisation. California boasts a string of superlatives. The mountains in the northeast, swathed in eternal ice, are amongst the highest on the continent. Death Valley in the southeast not only marks the lowest point in the US, but also the hottest. On the Pacific coast, trees reach higher into the sky than anywhere else. Some, such as the sequoias in the Sierra Nevada in the east, are amongst the oldest on the planet.

No other part of America has been praised as much as this, the *third-largest state in the US* after Alaska and Texas. There's more than enough of everything: mighty waterfalls in the Yosemite National Park and small picturesque towns along the coast, rough desert landscapes and fertile valleys, real whales in the ocean and artificial Mickey Mice in Disneyland. California has a low population density compared to the British Isles. Over half of California's 40 million inhabitants cluster around Los Angeles.

Endless supply of sun, sand and beach

Between Oregon in the north and Mexico in the south there's a lot of space for lonely mountain ranges, untouched forests and deserts devoid of people. Add to this the fact that the supply of sun, sand and beach seems to be endless. Where nature is so bountiful, the people are too, taking time to enjoy life. The *Californian lifestyle* is extremely easy-going and relaxed. The image of a happy-go-lucky leisure society – this is where it comes closest to the cliché: beach boys drive to the beach with their board in the car, to dance on the waves.

California was already enchanting as far back as 150 years ago when the *gold rush* pulled in 300,000 people from all corners of the earth. While precious few found the coveted precious metal, the new country offered everybody a chance – first with the construction of the railways, later in the oil business, and then, most of all, in agriculture. The growing *film industry* which settled in the early 20th century in Los Angeles made the American Dream *California-style* accessible to the

25,000–12,000 BC
Prehistoric Native American tribes settle California from the north

1542
Juan Rodríguez Cabrillo explores the waters north of Mexico

1769
Junípero Serra founds the first of 21 missions along the coast in San Diego

1812
Russian fur traders establish a post in northern California

1848
Mexico yields California to the USA. Large gold finds attract 300,000 fortune-seekers from all over the world

Jean Paul Getty collected around 50,000 artworks – most now on show at the Getty Museum

whole world. Today, *high-tech sectors* are constructing the future. California boasts the world's sixth-largest economy. However, the model of a lavish, lovable and liveable life has an underbelly too. The constant *drought conditions*

Pacemaker for environmental innovation

have had a detrimental effect on the economy and local lifestyles. The car-mad Californians produced one sprawling metropolis after the other, each exuding excitement and activity yet threatening nature. California, politically liberal and ecologically sensitive, couldn't fail to become a pacemaker for environmental innovation. The serious beginnings of producing energy using solar and wind power point the way to a future of alternative sources of power.

1850
California becomes the 31st federal state of the US

1869
The railway connects the eastern and western coast

1890
Thanks to the efforts of John Muir, the father figure of Californian environmentalists, the Yosemite Valley becomes a national park

1906
A disastrous earthquake destroys 28,000 houses in San Francisco

1911
The film industry establishes itself in Hollywood, producing its first moving picture in 1913

In years to come, energy and water will remain important buzzwords, as the population migrating to California, whether legally or illegally, are changing the *population structure*. These days, nearly 40 per cent of all Californians are considered *Hispanics* (the official denomination). This makes the time of Anglo-American domination appear nearly like an intermezzo. For in terms of colonial politics, *Baja* (i.e. lower) *California* and *Alta* (upper) *California* belonged to Mexico and were given independence, together with Mexico, by Spain in 1821. Americans pushing Pacific-wards from the east worked towards the secession of the northern part. In 1846, in the wake of the Mexican-American War, settlers founded the *California Republic*, which due to the bear on the flag has entered the history books as the *Bear Flag Republic*. In 1850, as the gold rush awakened Washington's interest in the lands far to the west, young California became the 31st state of the USA.

California: the Bear Flag Republic

When planning your visit think of the *distances* and the cultural idiosyncrasies of the regions. California is divided into three regions by geographic and tourist criteria. Each of them, and each metropolis, is worth a separate visit. If you want to get to know the variety of the state on a round trip, you can put together a selection of real highlights: in quiet North California, still lonely in parts, tranquil Pacific coves and virgin *redwood forests* await, as well as the fascinating *volcanic summits* of the Mount Shasta and Cascade ranges. In Central California, don't miss the drive along the breathtaking *coast* on Highway 1 between San Francisco and Los Angeles, and beyond the Central Valley the high alpine mountain world of the Sierra Nevada with its 3,000-year-old sequoias, famous *nature parks* such as Yosemite and *ghost towns* dating back to the times of the gold rush.

With *beaches*, *entertainment parks* and wildly romantic *deserts*, Southern California is an all-year round destination thanks to its southerly location. The interior shows its best side during the time of the desert bloom in March and April, but in the height of summer, the sun-scorched rocky deserts in Death Valley and the Mojave desert with temperatures topping 40°C/104°F and sometimes even 45 °C/113°F are to be enjoyed with caution. Immortalised by the Beach Boys' songs, the *surfing scene* on the beaches between San Diego and Los Angeles

1937
Inauguration of the Golden Gate Bridge

1941–45
San Francisco becomes the base for the Pacific fleet, Los Angeles develops a booming aircraft industry

1967
The hippie movement celebrates the Summer of Love in San Francisco

2008/09
Financial crisis, property prices nosedive

2018
California's deadliest and most destructive wildfires on record burn an area of nearly 1,500 mi²

Is this a cactus? No, it is a member of the lily family and has given its name to the Joshua Tree National Park

enjoys the easy life mainly in high summer and autumn, when the Pacific is warm enough to swim in. And winter is the best time for golfing in Palm Springs or walks in the otherwise burning-hot Death Valley. Last not least: the stimulating *super-cities of San Francisco* and *Los Angeles* are close enough together for you to get to know them in a single trip, but far enough apart to maintain their individual character: the innovative city on the Golden Gate presents a more European and cultured identity and is proud to be the cradle of the internet, Google and the iPad, while the entertainment metropolis a day trip further south is a glitzy

Stimulating super cities

hub for extroverts, show and glamour. What all this means is that California offers more than any other region in the US. But don't forget: to see a lot means covering great distances. To truly experience California, take your time.

It is therefore no wonder that California always was and still remains cosmopolitan, welcoming immigrants and visitors with new concepts and extra manpower. California is *not afraid of foreign cultures and influences*, instead absorbing innovative ideas and turning them into its own trends. It imported surfing from Hawaii and the film industry from the east coast, transformed Japanese sushi into the California Roll and developed inliners from the concept of European roller skates. Today, *the most creative individuals from all round the world* are flocking to Silicon Valley. Let's see what California will come up with next – a new type of sports equipment, a new food trend, a cool shopping idea or a hiking app. Keep your eyes open while you are travelling around.

WHAT'S HOT

1 More than sushi

Does Japanese food always mean sushi? Not necessarily. A new trend has reached California: *Izakaya,* the Japanese variant of the Spanish tapas bar which consists of delicious miniature dishes – not always with fish - which you can also share. *Yuzuki (598 Guerrero Street | www.yuzukisf. com)* in San Francisco for example serves meat on skewers, highly-spiced tofu and breast of duck. At *Sasaya (11613 Sante Monica Blvd. | www.izakaya-sasaya.com)* in L.A., you can try tasty belly of pork with crackling and roast ginko nuts.

Back to nature

2

Self-caterers The backyards of the cities are turning green. The neighbourhood residents dig up their own beds to grow vegetables in empty lots all over the place. Community gardens have even appeared in the concrete jungle of L.A., for example at Ocean View Farms *(3300 S Centinela Ave. | oceanview farms.net)*. The star of the scene is Novella Carpenter *(ghosttownfarm.wordpress.com)*, author of "Farm City: The Education of an Urban Farmer". She often gives talks, also at the Green Festivals *(www.greenfes tivals.org)*.

3 California fashion

Go local Oakland is home to designer Cari Borja, whose playful designs are finding fans worldwide. Her creations are available from her studio *(2117 4th Street | www.cariborja.com)*. On the other side of the bay, in San Francisco, Howard Gee specializes in custom-made jeans at his Atelier AB Fits *(1519 Grant Ave)*. At Colleen Quen *(131 8th Street | San Francisco | www.colleenquen couture.com)*, silk, brocade, and chiffon are the materials of choice for Quen's fancy frocks.

Cinematic workouts

Sporty fun Just sweating is not enough for body-conscious Californians. At *Crunch (8000 Sunset Blvd. | www.crunch.com)* in L.A. (also in other cities), courses such as "Power Yoga", "Powerwave Battle Roping" and "Washboard Abs" ensure ideal body measurements. Plus, they offer workouts according to the "Bodyshred" programme developed by the fitness guru Jillian Michaels. Even more courage is required for the workout at *Hollywood Aerial Arts (3838 W 102nd Street www.hollywoodaerialarts.com)* in Inglewood, who will shape your abdominals on the trapeze. Suffering from vertigo? Head for the Debbie Allen Dance *Academy (3791 Santa Rosalia Drive | Los Angeles | www.debbie allendanceacademy.com)* In addition to professional courses, the studio also offers regular open classes for teens and adults in ballet, hip-hop, Flamenco and just about every other kind of dance form.

Smart art

Party instead of punditry In San Francisco, even those who shirk galleries and museums can enjoy art. Cool parties and events put you in touch with your creative vibes. The parties at the Minna Gallery *(111 Minna Street www.111minnagallery.com)* (photo) are perfect. DJs, drinks and films help you take the first step. Another catalyst for easy art enjoyment is Adobe Books *(3130 24th Street | www.adobebooks.com)*. Since 2013, experimental performances and exhibits have made themselves at home in the new space in the Mission District. Live music and performances are also put on by the gallery Intersection of the Arts *(910 Mission Street | theintersection.org)*.

IN A NUTSHELL

ORGANIC FOOD

The magic word is 🌐 *organic,* better even *certified organic*, with a trustworthy quality seal. Since the days of the hippies, California has been a pioneer of today's ever-growing eco trend. Many towns have their own weekly *farmer's markets,* often only allowing *certified farmers*. One of the largest in northern California takes place every Saturday in summer on the plaza in the university town of Arcata near Eureka. For more markets see *www.cafarmers markets.com.*

Californians buy their organic cereals at the *health food store*. However, regular supermarkets too increasingly offer organic fare. And then there are the big new organic chains such as *Whole Foods* (www.wholefoodsmarket.com) or *Trader Joe's (www.traderjoes.com),* with ecologically correct products from Californian organic wine to sushi from sustainable sources. Few people realise that the owners Trader Joe's are actually European: the chain belongs to Aldi!

CALIFORNIA CRAZY

Beautiful is what pleases the eye: this is the motto Californians use in construction. A typically Californian style first emerged after the Second World War, when the diners and coffee shops were given huge windows and daringly overhanging roofs, while inside plump ketchup-red benches shone in the bright neon light. The name for this style was "Googie", and things carried on in this

California sets benchmarks for the world: both with big achievements and environmental problems

imaginative vein. A hamburger restaurant in the shape of a hamburger, the property firm Sphinx in a house modelled to resemble a sphinx, a dinosaur museum in a huge model dinosaur. Over the past few decades, California has turned itself into an architectural freestyle paradise. One which can easily accommodate the adventurous residential buildings made from redwood on the coast of northern California. "California Crazy" is the technical term for the most grotesque excesses.

California's skyscrapers, by the way, are all of more recent date. Only since it's been possible to build earthquake-safe buildings have architects started aiming for the sky. How high exactly is on show in the downtown district of Los Angeles, which for the past twenty years or so has been experiencing a building boom.

THE LAND IS PARCHED

Ever more frequently, Californians living in the south of the state are having their water supply cut off for a few hours a day. Together, Greater Los Angeles and San Diego, built into the desert and sprawling there unfettered, use up three quarters of all Californian supplies of drinking water. The question of how long Angelenos may still irrigate their lawns without thinking has been a political hot potato for years. The precious liquid is ferried in through the world's largest pipeline system – the Colorado River Aqueduct. It alone delivers over one billion US gallons of water a day! Los Angeles receives its water from the Sierra Nevada, nearly 400 km/249 mi away, from Lake Havasu, which also supplies San Diego, and from Sacramento Valley, 700 km/435 mi away.

SMOG

Los Angeles, city of freeways where the car rules, is infamous for its smog: for years, the American Lung Association has been warning of the worst air in the US. But there is an upside too. With the strictest environmental laws in the US, California is trying to tackle the air pollution in L.A., amongst other things. Smog levels were lowered by 75 per cent. You see more hybrid and electric cars now, and some car parks even have power points to refuel the emission-less little runabouts. And from the viewpoints on Mulholland Drive or the Getty Museum, L.A. can often be seen in amazingly clear panoramascope.

GRASS, POT & DOPE

On 8 November 2016, 56 per cent of Californians voted in favour of legalising marijuana as a recreational drug which would be just as legal to consume as alcohol and tobacco. This means that anyone over the age of 21 is permitted to possess and consume small quantities of *grass* – but not in public. How the sale of this drug is going to be regulated still has to be discussed as it is illegal to buy it on the street. The first marijuana shops and Amsterdam-styled coffee shops were due to open early in 2018. Although smok-

Black bears – like here in Sequoia National Park – sometimes have cinnamon-coloured fur

ing marijuana is accepted within private spheres, the consumption of harder drugs remains forbidden. Here, the californian drug fun ends and draconic fines are imposed.

GRIZZLIES & REDWOODS

Whilst the grizzly bear and the Californian condor have disappeared from the wild, California still provides a habitat for many threatened animals. The state that's home to 123 amphibians and reptilians, 260 species of bird and 27,000 different insects also allows to spot whales, sea lions, seals and sea otters along the coast. On land you might well see – with a little luck – lynxes, grey foxes, racoons, elk. And, at higher altitudes, mountain sheep, marmots and black bears.

The most conspicuous plants in California are the *redwoods* (at nearly 100 m/328 ft the world's tallest trees), *sequoias* (giant trees, at up to 30 m/98.4 ft diameter the largest living organisms in the world in terms of mass), palm trees, cacti and yucca plants such as the *Joshua trees,* which gave their name to an entire national park in southern California. Wildflowers blossom from spring to autumn in all colours. The mountains support lupines, lilies, asters and shepherd's purse, the desert more resistant shrubs such as the creosote bush with its olive-green leaves and yellow flowers.

HOLLYWOOD

When the first film companies settled in Hollywood, they laid the basis for an industry that has long since gone global – and way beyond the cinema business. In the 1950s, US television began using the expansive studio facilities created in the silent film era as production sites for the growing demand for TV series. Today, television is the most important branch of the Californian entertainment industry. Due to the increasing economic links between companies in the early 1970s, the big record labels too moved to the West Coast. The significance of the entertainment business for Los Angeles is demonstrated not only by the annual award ceremonies for Oscars, Grammys, Emmys and other honours for entertainment artists. With around 250,000 employees and countless junior talents hoping for their chance, show business is a big factor in the regional lifestyle. It's visible not least in the super-rich who have built themselves veritable dream mansions behind high walls in Beverly Hills and Malibu.

NATIVE AMERICANS

Possessing no written language and no metal, America's original inhabitants have left few indicators as to their culture, apart from cave paintings and some masterfully woven baskets today kept in museums. The first Europeans landing on California's coasts by boat received a cordial welcome. The Miwoks, for instance, graced Sir Francis Drake, when he set foot on land, with a crown of feathers.

From 1770 onwards, the coastal tribes near the Spanish missions were decimated by diseases they caught from the settlers such as measles, chickenpox and syphilis. The settlers coming in from the east pushed back the inland Indians, and encountered some resistance. In the mountains of northeast California, for example, the Modocs fought a guerrilla war against US troops over several years – in vain. By 1870, nearly 90 per cent of the Indigenous inhabitants had been annihilated, and the survivors placed in small reservations on inferior land. Their descendants still live there, many of them – such as the Cahuila at Palm Springs, the Paiute Shoshone in Owens Valley and the Hupa on the northern coast – keeping themselves very much to themselves. However, many of the 400,000 Californian Native Americans live in the big cities too.

KARL THE FOG

The summer fog on the coast of California is legendary – and notorious. There is hardly an image of the Golden Gate Bridge without it. The cold water of the Pacific takes a long time to warm up in the spring and inland temperatures can rise swiftly to 40°C/104°F and above. These high air temperatures meeting low sea temperatures is the cause of the coastal fog which hangs around San Diego in June and San Francisco in July. By September, the fog disappeares and temperatures stabilise. Naturally, San Francisco has its own idiosyncratic name for the fog collecting around the Golden Gate which is known as Karl and has a presence on social media: *@KarlTheFog* entertains its 200,000 followers on Twitter with witty stements along the lines of "In fog we trust", "Blue sky, you will be mist" and the weather forecast "Foggy with a high chance of ordering pizza".

NATIONAL PARKS

Nine of the 59 American national parks are situated in California: Channel Islands, Death Valley, Joshua Tree, Kings Canyon, Lassen Volcanic, Pinnacles, Redwood, Sequoia and Yosemite. These conservation areas are vital to the survival of many of the state's 260 species of birds, over 100 reptiles and amphibians as well as whales, sea lions, grey foxes and black bears, protected by a massive army of *rangers*. Serving wildlife conservation, these territories allow 280 million visitors per year (over the whole of the US) to observe the wonders of nature and the geological development of the earth close up.

The stronger the environmental idea became, the more areas were placed under

PATENT 139.121

When Levi Strauss – born in 1847 in southern Germany – arrived in New York, he couldn't have known that his name would become a brand. For six years he went to San Francisco, with the idea of supplying the gold prospectors. One of his partners was the tailor Jacob Davis, who bulk-bought tear-resistant fabric from Levi. Coloured blue using indigo, the fabric imported by Strauss at the time would often come from France, more specifically, Nîmes. Hence the name "denim", "de Nîmes". As one of their clients constantly tore his pockets, Davis one day hit on the idea of reinforcing all seams and pockets with metal rivets. These "studded pants" became an immediate hit with the gold miners. However, Davis lacked the money to have his idea patented, the patent office asking for $68. Davis approached Levi Strauss, asking for help. The latter immediately recognised the potential of the new type of trousers and came on board. On 20 May 1873, the two men were awarded patent no. 139.121 by the Patent and Trademark Office – and blue jeans were born.

This is a tough climb, but the view over the peaks of Yosemite National Park is astounding

protection as *National Monuments,* and taken away from private use as *National Forests* worthy of protection or as *National Recreation Areas.* An *America the Beautiful Annual Pass* for $80 gives the passholder plus one car and three passengers a year of free entry to all parks and other federal conservation areas. For more information see *www.nps.gov.*

SUSTAINABILITY

Sustainability is the new buzzword with California's eco activists. While the Washington-based federal government is rather hesitant in terms of protecting the environment, the state and many cities in California have started their own green initiatives. San Francisco for instance was the first city in America to ban plastic bags, and since 2011 the city's taxis are either hybrid vehicles or run on bio fuel. Many restaurants will only serve fish caught sustainably, with scientists working at the Monterey Bay Aquarium issuing a constantly updated list. Public buildings and hotels are increasingly built according to so-called *LEED standards*, LEED standing for *Leadership in Energy and Environmental Design,* the particularly strict rules and regulations of the US Green Building Council, *www.usgbc.org.*

THE BIG ONE

The western coast sits right on top of the *"Ring of Fire",* a volcanic and earthquake-prone zone around the Pacific. The friction of the tectonic plates at the continent's edge produces jerky movements that become noticeable on the surface as earthquakes.

The worst quakes to date on California's most famous fault line, the San Andreas Fault, happened in 1857 in Los Angeles, and in 1906 and 1989 in San Francisco. There were quakes of medium impact in the north of Los Angeles (1994) and more recently in Napa Valley (2014). Geologists reckon that a major disaster, *"The Big One",* is still to come.

FOOD & DRINK

California is America's tasting kitchen for a new gastronomic awareness. Take excellent base ingredients, new and evolving recipes, mix in some chutzpah and season it with as many prominent guests as possible.

Whether Bavarian veal sausage next to Moroccan lamb, salsa made with yellow tomatoes next to caviar pizza – food *à la californienne* always need a bit of show and new sensations.

This is how some 40 years ago *fusion* or *California cuisine* was born. Its main characteristics have stayed the same to this day: cook lightly, use the ethnic specialities of varied peoples who have come to your country and get all ingredients on local markets. Constant innovation and new creations are the name of the game.

More and more *market-conscious restaurants* meet this demand. Following the success of *Spago* in L.A., Wolfgang Puck opened *Chinois* in Santa Monica, plus a whole chain of *Wolfgang Puck Restaurants*. Joachim Splichal, who now owns a couple of dozen restaurants scattered across the US, runs *Patina* in downtown L.A. as well as Café Pinot, and also the café at the LACMA Museum in Las Vegas. Daring culinary links across continents, such as Mexican-Thai or Franco-Japanese, are also finding their fans. Puck calls this kind of *cooking "multicultural"*. The Californian joy in innovations like this has long inspired chefs all over the US.

The *cradle of California cuisine* however stands in San Francisco. In around 1970 Alice Waters, head chef at *Chez Panisse*

Multiculturally inspired creations, health-conscious wholefoods, or a good ol' steak – try them all and see what you like

(1517 Shattuck Ave. | tel. 510 5 48 55 25 | Expensive | less pricey bistro on upper floor) in Berkeley, first elevated cooking with regional products to be the most important principle of the new Californian cuisine.

The excellent quality and the enormous variety of California's agricultural produce underpin the efforts of its **innovative chefs**. The mild climate and good soil of Central Valley east of San Francisco allows fruits such as nuts and peaches to thrive as much as rice, corn or melons. Vegetables and tomatoes grow all year round.

The southern deserts provide grapefruit, dates and oranges, the pastures of northern California steaks, fine cheeses and other dairy products. No wonder that in agricultural production California is the leader amongst all US states.

The latest trend is ◐ **organic food**. Many well-educated Californians, in the San Francisco area in particular, buy their organic produce from *farmer's markets* and organic supermarkets. Even the *street food* scene of hot dogs and burgers is following the trend –

LOCAL SPECIALITIES

blackened mahimahi – common dolphin fish, seared (with a black crust)

Caesar salad with chicken strips – salad with a parmesan-anchovy dressing and strips of chicken

California roll – avocado and crab meat Japanese-style in a rice roll (photo right)

eggs sunny side up with bacon and hash browns – the breakfast classic: fried eggs with crispy bacon and pan-fried grated potatoes

filet mignon with baked potato – fillet steak with jacket potato in aluminium foil

fish taco with cilantro – tortilla shell with grilled fish, seasoned with coriander

French toast with maple syrup – sliced bread in an egg batter (eggy bread) with maple syrup

honey lager microbrew – lager from a microbrewery, partly brewed using honey, partly only named for its light-brown colour

nachos with guacamole and sour cream – Mexican corn chips with a baked cheese topping, served with avocado dip and sour cream (photo left)

New York steak with stuffed mushrooms – steak with a trim of fat, served with oven-baked filled large portabello mushrooms

prime rib with horseradish sauce – very tender chunky slice of roast (the best meat off the beef), served with the hot sauce

pumpkin pie – the American classic, not just for Halloween

seared tuna with sesame crust – a typical Californian combination of flavours

sirloin steak with corn on the cob – another American classic

strawberry margarita – cocktail made from strawberries, crushed ice and tequila

turkey with stuffing, yams and cranberry sauce – a variation on the classic festive dish

often, the *all-beef sausages* are even *certified organic,* i.e. tested by independent laboratories. Some snack stalls now offer true gourmet fare – easy to recognise, as at lunch break the queue extends all around the block.

Increasing interest in fine creative dishes goes hand in hand with a rising number of connoisseurs of reputable *Californian wines*. In the most important winegrowing areas of Napa Valley and Sonoma Valley, countless new winemak-

FOOD & DRINK

Organic markets are all the rage

ers have reverted to the good old European way of doing things. For a long time, varietal, i.e. non-blended wines had no market in the US. Only when wine drinkers were prepared to adapt their palates to grapes such as Chardonnay and Sauvignon Blanc (white) or Cabernet Sauvignon and Zinfandel (red), were ambitious winemakers such as Robert Mondavi and Andre Tchelistcheff confirmed in their efforts. One reason for the high quality is the climate. Unlike in Europe, winemakers can harvest fully ripened grapes that develop a stronger flavour. This flavour is then rounded off by storage in oak barrels.

Alongside the trend towards more culinary refinement, which of course comes with the requisite price tag, there is down-to-earth American fare too, with some excellent **barbecue dishes**. Near the coast, fresh fish is a good choice. Inland why not go for the obligatory steak with a baked Idaho potato or a hamburger – unless it's from a fast-food chain. Meat (and tuna steaks) can be cooked

according to your wishes: *rare*, *medium rare* and *well done*.

Whether in the big cities or in the provinces, many Americans start their day with a **breakfast in a coffee shop** or at a diner. Coffee is served *bottomless*, i.e. with free refills, to complement eggs, bacon and toast. On the road, a great filling and cheap choice are the *truck stops* used by the long-distance drivers.

All restaurants have a *lunch menu* with sandwiches and soups, at prices substantially below those of the *dinner menu*. Americans often drink *ice tea* or coffee with their lunch. Beer is also popular. Very trendy: beer from privately run *microbreweries*, is sure to please the palates of European visitors. In rural areas in particular, *dinner* starts being served from 5 or 5.30pm onwards, and usually only up to 9pm. And last not least, a word about the bill, or rather, the check as Americans call it: **VAT** is not included in the prices shown on the menu, nor is the **tip**, which for the waiting staff constitutes a major part of their income.

SHOPPING

Since the Californians renovated and revived their city centres, going shopping has become a lot of fun. The city centre of San Diego around the stylish and original *Horton Plaza, State Street* in Santa Barbara with its pretty Spanish courtyards, the *Ferry Building Market Place* and hip *Union Street* in San Francisco... but the *Third Street Promenade* in Santa Monica with its *Mall Santa Monica Place*, the kooky *Melrose Avenue* and the elegant *Grove Shopping Center* in Los Angeles are the most rewarding shopping strips, with plenty of California flair included.

CAMPING SUPPLIES

Travelling around California by hire car gives you opportunities to stock up on basics everywhere. Convenience stores such as 7–11 or *Circle K* or small shops in hotels and at petrol stations sell drinks and ice cubes for the cool box, coffee and doughnuts, snacks and newspapers. Drugstores not only sell cosmetics, but also often medication from an in-house pharmacy. And whatever you may need, huge supermarkets such as *Albertson's, Safeway* or *Walmart* leave no wishes unfulfilled.

For good organic food, there are chains such as Whole Foods. Be aware that at the till all prices are subject to a sales tax of at least 7.5 per cent, which depending on the region, can climb to 10 per cent.

CRAFTS

Many arts and crafts fairs stock innovative costume jewellery, colourful ceramics, woodwork and other crafts. Markets like this, where you can often buy direct from the artists, can be found at weekends in Gold Country and the coastal towns in particular. These towns also boast numerous galleries specialising in crafts.

Indian crafts such as turquoise jewellery or traditional pottery are usually made in Arizona or New Mexico. The Californian tribes make small baskets from sweetgrass or bead-embroidered moccasins.

OUTLET MALLS

A popular choice for discount shopping are the numerous outlet malls selling big brands such as Levi's, Timberland, Calvin Klein or Tommy Hilfiger direct-

Shopping – an all-American pastime in shopping centres, on markets and in outlet malls

ly to the customer. These outlets are usually located outside the cities on Interstate highways, e.g. at Cabazon on the I-10, at Barstow on the I-15 or at Vacaville on the I-80 between San Francisco and Sacramento. Not least because of the constant special sales, the outlets may have excellent bargains, and sometimes stores offer additional discount coupons. You can find out more from the service desk of the centre you're visiting.

TYPICAL SOUVENIRS

Californian products make lovely gifts. A bottle of a wine from a hidden winery, seeds of redwood trees, salsa spice mix or honey from desert flowers. Cuttings taken from cacti will carry on growing at home. While in the wild, these prickly souvenirs are strictly protected, many garden centres sell good-value offshoots all wrapped up ready for export. What else is worth looking for? Apart from clothes by trendy brands such as Hollister, Abercrombie & Fitch or American Eagle, used and new leather jackets (bomber jacket-style, also available from army and navy stores), jeans and outdoor gear, vintage clothing from the 1950s that you can sometimes discover on large flea markets (*swap meets*).

Also popular are all products that have their roots in cowboy culture – even if this is more typical of the Rocky Mountain area. A broad selection of Stetson hats, silver-studded belts and good cowboy boots can be found in many western stores.

Other items significantly cheaper than in Europe include sports gear such as golf equipment, as well as all kinds of vitamin supplements and power drinks. Be aware that customs officials will immediately recognise large new purchases for what they are on your return, so it's better to declare purchases with a value of over $508.

SAN FRANCISCO

CITY **WHERE TO START?**
Union Square (U F2) (*⌖ f2*)
is the heart of the city. Here you can
shop, get on a cable car or walk on
through Chinatown to the Coit Tower
and Fisherman's Wharf. The Museum of Modern Art and Market
Street, served by buses, Metro, cable
cars and the F Line, is not far either.
Multi-storey car park: Mission Street
between 4th and 5th Street

MAP INSIDE BACK COVER
(134 A1) (*⌖ B7*) Ask most Americans which city they'd most like to visit, and the reply is likely to be: San
Francisco. This popularity is well founded, as truly no other metropolis in the
US packs so much charm within so little space. Life in this city – which the locals lovingly call the "Lady by the Bay"
– is vibrant: it's busy but not hectic, cultured but not arrogant.

Built on 40 small and seven big hills on
the northern point of a narrow peninsula sheltering the large Bay, today around
870,000 people live in the city, which is
the powerhouse for the entire Bay region with its 8.7 million inhabitants. Two
bridges (Golden Gate Bridge and San
Francisco-Oakland Bay Bridge, remodelled as recently as 2013), a subway and
countless ferries connect the people on
each side of the Bay.

San Francisco is easy to explore on foot.
Start at the Waterfront. The idea here is

Photo: 'Painted Ladies ': Victorian houses at Alamo Square

America's most beautiful city: the gem on the Pacific and city of dreams – not only for Americans

to explore tourist hotspots such as the famous Fisherman's Wharf, the Mediterranean-looking Marina District and the Golden Gate Promenade leading to the Presidio, the former barracks under eucalyptus trees.

Very important too are the city centre and its adjacent neighbourhoods: North Beach, the Italian quarter with its cafés, restaurants and gelaterias. Then Nob Hill, the fancy neighbourhood set on the hills, as well as Russian Hill and Pacific Heights, where every street offers fabulous views of the Bay. Chinatown, the largest of its kind in North America, lies south of North Beach. Around Union Square, the heart of Downtown, the cable cars sound their bells and hotels, theatres and department stores await. Last but not least is the Castro District, the gay quarter. Next to it find the Mexican Mission District and South of Market, neglected for a long time, but today a cultural hotspot with galleries, museums and exciting nightlife. You can save expensive parking fees by using public buses, trams, cable cars

Genius energy-saving concept of the 19th century: the cable cars

or the INSIDER TIP historic tram carriages from all over the world of the F Line *(daily 6am–0.30am | $2.50, cable cars $7, day pass $21 | can be bought in the bus or train itself | app MuniMobile)*. You can take the F line to travel from Market Street via the Ferry Building along the Bay to Fisherman's Wharf. Combine the journey with a trip back (or there) by one of the cable cars to turn this into a proper city sightseeing tour.

SIGHTSEEING

ALCATRAZ ISLAND ⚓ **(134 A1)** *(𝄞 B7)*
Only nine prisoners ever succeeded in escaping from Alcatraz which provided the inspiration for a number of Hollywood films. *The Rock*, the prison on the island, was considered the most secure in the world. During the period between 1934 and 1963, notorious criminals such as Al Capone were interned here, frequently on long sentences. Today, a visit including a boat trip lasts only 2.5 hours.

Departures: Pier 33 at the eastern end of Fisherman's Wharf **(U F1)** *(𝄞 f1) | departures daily from 8.45am, night tours available too | ticket $37.25 | tel. 1 415 9 81 76 25 | www.alcatrazcruises.com | pre-book well in advance!*

INSIDER TIP **ASIAN ART MUSEUM**
(U E2–3) *(𝄞 e2–3)*
Over 17,000 objects from China, Japan, India, Nepal, Tibet and Southeast Asia, many of them donated by former IOC president Avery Brundage. One of the best Asian museums of the western world. Good shop. *Tue–Sun 10am–5pm, Thu until 9pm | admission $15 | 200 Larkin Street | www.asianart.org*

CABLE CARS ★ ⚓
Pulled by cables for over 100 years now, the streetcar is an icon of the city. *The Powell-Mason line* starts at Hallidie Plaza, winds its way up into the wealthy neighbourhood of Nob Hill, then descends again on Mason Street to near Fish-

erman's Wharf. *The Powell-Hyde Line:* Market/Powell Street to Northern Waterfront. California Line: California Street from Market Street to Van Ness Avenue. An impressive sight in the freely accessible centre of operations, the ● *Cable Car Museum (see p. 117)* (U E2) (⑪ e2), are the massive pinions that move cable cars.

CALIFORNIA ACADEMY OF SCIENCES
● ⊕(U C3) (⑪ c3)
Star architect Renzo Piano has designed the new building of the huge natural history museum with the most modern green technologies – complete with rainforest and organic shapes. Pride of place in the complex is given over to the Steinhart Aquarium. *Mon–Sat 9.30am–5pm, Sun 11am–5pm | admission $35 | Golden Gate Park | www.calacademy.org*

CHINATOWN ★ (U E–F2) (⑪ e–f2)
Grant Avenue, today full of import businesses and souvenir shops, was formerly the street of opium dens, gambling houses and brothels. You can already sense the exotic atmosphere when you enter through the dragon gate with its pagoda roof on Bush Street. Stockton Street is considered the second main street of Chinatown. Over 100 restaurants cluster between Stockton and Bush Streets alone, as well as Kearny and Broadway (our tip: Hunan *(924 Sansome Street | tel. 1 415 9 56 77 27 | Moderate)* and Dol Ho *(808 Pacific Street | tel. 1 415 3 92 28 28 | Budget–Moderate)*. Also worth a visit is the pagoda-shaped Old Chinese Telephone Exchange (743 Washington Street) and Buddha's Universal Church (720 Washington Street). Lured by the gold rush, the first fortune seekers from China came around 1850. A few years later many of them were being used as coolies for the construction of the railway. In recent times, refugees have further swelled the ranks of Chinese in the western US.

CIVIC CENTER (U E3) (⑪ e3)
The cultural and political centre of San Francisco is situated between not very salubrious neighbourhoods, Tenderloin and Western Addition: *City Hall*, a

---

★ Cable Cars
A rattling experience in historic trams: take the cable car down Hyde Street to Fisherman's Wharf and hang on for dear life → p. 34

★ Chinatown
Exotic scents and delicious restaurants in the oldest Chinese settlement outside Asia → p. 35

★ Coit Tower
The tip of a firefighters' coil as the emblem of the city – with a fantastic view → p. 36

★ Golden Gate Bridge
The fog-shrouded symbol of San Francisco – a technical masterpiece → p. 37

★ Golden Gate Park
Green fields, great museums, festivals and a lot of hippie history → p. 37

★ SoMa (South of Market)
It's all action here, and not only at night → p. 41

★ Ferry to Sausalito
A trip involving water, wind and a view of the skyline and Golden Gate → p. 43

MARCO POLO HIGHLIGHTS

domed granite and marble building, at its back the *Veteran's Building*, where in 1945 the charter of the United Nations was signed, next door the *War Memorial Opera House* with one of the best opera ensembles in the world, the San Francisco Opera, and the more modern edifice of the *Symphony Hall*.

COIT TOWER ★ ᔥ (U F1) (*ⵍ f1*)

The cylindrical viewing tower, 63 m/ 206.7 ft high, was erected in 1933 by Lillie Hitchcock Coit on the summit of 74 m/ 242.8 ft Telegraph Hill in honour of San Francisco's firefighters. Coit Tower offers an excellent view of the city and the bay. *Daily 10am–6pm, in the winter 10am– 5pm | elevator $8 | Telegraph Hill*

CONTEMPORARY JEWISH MUSEUM (U F2) (*ⵍ f2*)

For this museum, opened in 2008, Daniel Libeskind placed one of his typical crystal shapes into the urban landscape. With its inclined walls, the interior space has a very calming effect. *Thu–Tue 11am–5pm, Thu until 8pm | admission $14 | 736 Mission Street*

CRISSY FIELD ᔥ (U C1) (*ⵍ c1*)

The last piece of real dune landscape left on the city's northern coast – a pretty setting for a bike tour or a beach walk on the Bay with an unimpeded view of the pelicans sailing the wind currents off the Golden Gate Bridge. *Along Old Mason Street | www.parksconservancy.org*

DE YOUNG MUSEUM (U C3) (*ⵍ c3*)

The city's most important art museum resides in an extensive building that cost 200 million dollars and was designed by Swiss architects Herzog & de Meuron. The emphasis of the exhibitions is on American art. Don't miss ᔥ INSIDER**TIP** the tower with a platform for views across the city, sculpture garden and café. *Tue– Sun 9.30am–5.15pm | admission $10 | Golden Gate Park | www. famsf.org*

EXPLORATORIUM (U F1) (*ⵍ f1*)

This famous science museum moved into its big new home on the Bay in 2013. Children as well as adults love to explore the interactive exhibits that peak your curiosity and let you experiment with science in a playful way. *Tue–Sun 10am–5pm, Thu until 10pm | admission $29 | Embarcadero | Pier 15 | www.exploratorium.edu*

FERRY BUILDING (U F2) (*ⵍ f2*)

Unusual speciality shops, food stalls and restaurants are housed in the highly decorated ferry building dating from 1898 which today is a modern market hall presenting the great variety of Calilfornian cuisine. The *Farmers' Market* held on Saturdays in the Plaza on the shore of the bay is a popular attraction. In the evening, you should not miss looking over at the *Oakland Bay Bridge* which is illuminated by thousands of LED lamps as part of the art project INSIDER**TIP** *Bay Lights*. *Market Street | Embarcadero*

FISHERMAN'S WHARF ᔥ (U E1) (*ⵍ e1*)

The jetty once used by the Bay fishermen is crawling with street artists and T-shirt shops. It's from here that the boats depart for cruises around the Bay and to the Golden Gate Bridge. A word of warning: many of the restaurants here are overpriced. At *Pier 39*, lined by shops and viewpoints, a colony of sea lions which has colonised several pontoons offers a now famous photo opportunity.

A bit further west, at the end of Taylor Street/Pier 45, the INSIDER**TIP** Musée Mécanique is well worth a visit with its wonderfully nostalgic exhibition of old jukeboxes and games machines.

GOLDEN GATE BRIDGE ★ ⚘
(U C1) (🕮 c1)

The world's most-photographed suspension bridge! It has connected the northern point of San Francisco and Marin County since 1937. Two pillars jutting out 230 m/755 ft above the water surface carry a six-lane roadway spanning 1,280 m/4,200 ft at an average 67 m/219.8 ft above the water. ● You can cycle across on a hire bike. Tackling the bridge on foot is also well worthwhile – this takes about two hours there and back *(starting from the last stop of the Muni bus no. 28)*. Standing below the bridge looking up (a good view can be enjoyed from the ⚘ *Fort Point National Historic Site*, it was built in 1850 to protect the Golden Gate Passage) is breathtaking.

GOLDEN GATE PARK ★
(U A–C3) (🕮 a–c3)

This park spanning an area of 1.5 mi² as far as the Pacific with its Frisbee fields, paths for cyclists and rollerbladers, festivals and colourful gardens is a favourite playground for San Franciscans, particularly at the weekend. It has now also lost its hippy image from the legendary Summer of Love in 1967 – marijuana clouds above the meadows prove the point.

The *Japanese Tea Garden* in the eastern part of the park has acquired worldwide fame as an emblem of the city. You'll also find several museums here, as well as the splendidly renovated *Conservatory of Flowers*, a filigree white hothouse in the style of London's Kew Gardens.

INSIDERTIP ▶ HAYES VALLEY
(U E3) (🕮 e3)

The city's latest trendy neighbourhood lies directly behind City Hall along Hayes Street. By citizens' decree, chain stores were prohibited (even Starbucks), so here you'll see a cluster of fun shoe and clothes shops, eccentric galleries and individual bars and restaurants such as the breakfast diner *Stack's (501 Hayes Street)*. That San Francisco is the west

Fascinating! Meso-American culture and more besides in the De Young Museum

coast's prime city of jazz also becomes evident here: In 2013, the new *Jazz Center (210 Franklin Street | www.sfjazz.org)* opened behind San Francisco's symphony hall with several concert halls where something is on almost daily, and an excellent small tapas restaurant.

Lombard Street – the craziest serpentine road in the world

LOMBARD STREET (U E1) *(𝄞 e1)*
Nowhere in the whole of California are more photos taken: America's most crooked street, planted with flowers and framed by Victorian villas. *Only a few paces from Fisherman's Wharf between Leavenworth and Hyde Street*

MISSION DOLORES PARK ☼
(U E4) *(𝄞 e4)*
The park next to the small adobe-style church at the northern end of the mission district – it once was the heart of the city – is a favourite picnic and festival spot today, offering a fantastic view of the city skyline. *Dolores Street/18th Street*

SAN FRANCISCO MARITIME NATIONAL HISTORIC PARK (U E1) *(𝄞 e1)*
Marvel at the history of seafaring, explained using old schooners and steamboats at Hyde Street Pier *(Hyde Street | west of Fisherman's Wharf)*. Inside the museum are exhibits from the history of seafaring and fishing. *Daily 9.30am–5pm | admission $10 | 900 Beach Street | Polk Street*

SAN FRANCISCO MUSEUM OF MODERN ART (SFMOMA) (U F2) *(𝄞 f2)*
This is the most spectacular temple of modern art in the city, particularly since 2016 when the extension by Snohetta was opened, thereby doubling the exhibition area of the otherwise post-modern building. More space was vital in view of the almost 30,000 works in the collection which Includes a photography centre. *Thu 10am–9pm, Fri-Tue 10am–5pm | Admission 25$ | 151 3rd Street | Ticket reservation recommended: www.sfmoma.org.*

INSIDER TIP ▸ YERBA BUENA GARDENS ☼ (U F2) *(𝄞 f2)*
What a great surprise: a peaceful green space at the heart of the city! Plus, good views of the skyline. The small park com-

plex also houses a theatre, numerous sculptures, the *Martin Luther King, Jr. Memorial, Fountain & Waterfall* as well as the *Children's Creativity Museum* (see p. 117).

SIGHTSEEING TOURS

49-MILE SCENIC DRIVE

The route is indicated by signs featuring a seagull: an 80 km/49.7 mi tour taking you past all major attractions and scenic viewpoints in the metropolitan area of the city - a great day trip in a rented car. *Starts at the Civic Center*

BAY CITY BIKE

A wonderful half-day tour also suitable for children: a guided bike tour across the Golden Gate Bridge, back by ferry from Sausalito. You can also hire your own bikes if you want to undertake the tour independently (which is unproblematic). *2661 Taylor Street | Fisherman's Wharf | tel. 1 415 3 46 24 53 | www.baycitybike.com*

BOAT TRIPS (U F1) (⬚ f1)

For the classic *Golden Gate Bay Cruise*, lasting a good hour, board a boat of the *Red and White Fleet ($32 | Embarcadero | tel. 1 415 6 73 29 00)* from Pier 43½ or the *Blue & Gold Fleet (departure at Pier 39 | tel. 1 415 7 05 82 00)*.

ELECTRIC TOUR COMPANY

Three-hour Segway tours along Fisherman's Wharf – for advanced users also on the steep hills of the city. *757 Beach Street | tel. 1 415 4 74 31 30 | www.electrictourcompany.com*

INSIDER TIP HAIGHT-ASHBURY FLOWER POWER WALKING TOUR

This tour through the former hippie neighbourhood of Haight-Ashbury includes the houses of Janis Joplin and the Grateful Dead. *Tue and Sat 10.30am,*

Fri 2pm | $20 for a two-hour tour | starting point: corner Stanyan/Waller Street | www.haightashburytour.com.

SAN FRANCISCO SIGHTSEEING CO.

2.5 hour city tours (daily 9am-6pm | $48) on a hop-on, hop-off bus with 20 stops plus excursions to Napa and Monterey. *Departure from Pier 39 | Fisherman's Wharf | tel. 1888 4 28 69 37 | www.sanfranciscosightseeing.com*

WOKWIZ TOURS

Well-informed walks through Chinatown including lunch in one of the

LOW BUDGET

Muni Passports give you the freedom of the whole city on tram and buses: 1 day costs $21, 3 days $32, 7 days $42; regular fare is $2.50, cable car $7. *www.sfmta.com*

If you're planning on doing a lot of sightseeing, consider getting the CityPass San Francisco; $89 buys you a harbour cruise and admission to the DeYoung Museum or the Exploratorium and the California Academy of Sciences as well as the Muni Passport for one week. Or the GO San Francisco Card *(www.smartdestinations.com)* will get you discounted admission to up to 26 attractions.

Would you like to know more about the Castro District, the gold rush, or the earthquake of 1906? No problem! For the past 30 years City Guides volunteers have been offering daily free walking tours through the city. Schedule at *www.sfcityguides.org*.

restaurants. *Daily 10am | ticket $50 | tel. 650 3 55 96 57 | www.wokwiz.com*

FOOD & DRINK

Streetfood is also a trend in San Fransisco: Mexican, Aisan and American styles! Around a dozen mobile food trucks are located at different locations each day throughout the city – these locations often end up as a party: e.g. on Sunday evenings at Presidio and Saturdays at Fort Mason. Up-to-date information regarding locations can be found on the internet. *offthegridsf.com*.

INSIDER TIP ARIZMENDI BAKERY (U C3) (*m c3*)
San Francisco's response to the fast-food mania: a bakery just south of Golden Gate Park, which belongs to the employees and sells tasty breads, pizzas and focaccias. *1331 9th Ave. (also 1268 Valencia Street | www.arizmendibakery.org | Budget*

B RESTAURANT (U F2) (*m f2*)
From the terrace or behind the huge glass frontage, the view of the city's skyline really opens up. Californian cuisine. *Yerba Buena Center | 720 Howard Street | tel. 1 415 4 95 98 00 | Moderate*

FARALLON (U E2) (*m e2*)
The finest fish, some of it presented imaginatively. Another extraordinary touch: the octopus-shaped bar stools. *450 Post Street/Mason Street | tel. 1 4 15 9 56 69 69 | www.farallonrestaurant. com | Expensive*

INSIDER TIP PUERTO ALEGRE (U E3) (*m e3*)
Authentic Mexican cuisine and good Margaritas in the trendy Mission District. *546 Valencia Street | tel. 1 415 2 55 82 01 | Budget–Moderate*

SAM'S GRILL (U F2) (*m f2*)
A classic: fish, fresh mussels and crabs along a popular restaurant mile. Good lunch spot. *374 Bush Street | tel. 1 415 4 21 05 94 | Moderate–Expensive*

THIRSTY BEAR (U F2) (*m f2*)
Trendy brewery pub serving eco beer and fabulously tasty tapas. *661 Howard Street | tel. 1 415 9 74 09 05 | Moderate–Expensive*

YANK SING (U F2) (*m f2*)
A fantastic selection of tasty dim sum on the edge of the Financial District. *49 Stevenson Street | tel. 1 415 5 41 49 49 | Budget*

SHOPPING

San Francisco's shopping scene is less about huge malls than thousands of small high-quality shops, often with a unique selection. Department stores and boutiques cluster in the following neighbourhoods: the area around *Union Square* is the shopping heart of Downtown, with the famous department stores like Macy's and Neiman Marcus and luxury brands such as Hermès and Gucci. The *San Francisco Center (865 Market Street/Powell Street)* with the Nordstrom department store and 35 shops, as well as the *Crocker Galleria (50 Post Street/Kearny Street)* with 50 shops and restaurants are situated right in the heart of the action.

Other shopping hotspots are Union Street between Fillmore Street and Van Ness Street (shoes, fashion), Fillmore Street between Jackson Street and Sutter Street (boutiques and galleries), Hayes Street west of City Hall (avant-garde boutiques), Haight Street between Stanyan Street and Central Avenue (hip citywear, antiques). For your fresh produce pick a Saturday to head for the **INSIDER TIP** *Farmer's*

Market at the Ferry Building to find exclusively products from organic agriculture – add to that numerous snack food stalls offering tacos with organic meat, vegan pizzas and organic pastries.

AMOEBA MUSIC (U D3) *(📂 d3)*
You won't find new CDs and old vinyl records any cheaper than in this humungous music store in the former hippie quarter. *1855 Haight Street | www.amoeba.com*

GOLDEN GATE FORTUNE COOKIE COMPANY (U F2) *(📂 f2)*
Small, slightly hidden shop producing Chinese fortune cookies – you can watch and buy direct from them. *56 Ross Alley/ Jackson Street*

R & J GIFTS (U E1) *(📂 e1)*
Signs, baseball caps with logos, magnets and all those other typical American souvenirs that you've been looking for. *2633 Taylor Street*

The best addresses for hot nightlife are the former factory complex of ★ *SoMa (South of Market)* and the gay bars in the *Castro* neighbourhood and on *Folsom Street* (U E3–F2) *(📂 e3–f2)*. The bars and clubs of the Financial District (U F2) *(📂 f2)* and *Union Street* (U D2) *(📂 d2)* are hunting grounds of the urban elite. Back in the day, the famous coffee bars on Columbus Street (U E1–F2) *(📂 e1–f2)* in North Beach were frequented by Jack Kerouac *(in Vesuvio, no. 255)* and Francis Ford Coppola.

For current events also check the San Francisco Weekly, the San Francisco Guardian and the Sunday edition of the San Francisco Examiner, but also online under *www.sfweekly.com, www.sfbg.com, www.sfgate.com.*

CAFÉ DU NORD (U D3) *(📂 d3)*
Live jazz, salsa, lounge music, with tapas to keep you going. *2174 Market Street/ Sanchez Street | tel. 1 415 4 71 29 69 | www.cafedunord.com*

In-your-face fashion, hip neighbourhood: Haight-Ashbury

THE FILLMORE (U D2) *(📂 d2)*
Legendary concert stage, where the best bands in the States have performed. *1805 Geary Blvd. | tickets: tel. 1 800 7 45 30 00 | thefillmore.com*

EL TECHO DE LOLINDA (U E4) *(📂 e4)*
On the roof terrace the chic scene meets for margaritas. They also serve tapas (e.g. ceviche with mangos) – or substantial steaks on the ground floor. *2516 Mission Street | tel. 1 415 5 50 69 70 | eltechosf.com*

RUBY SKYE (U E2) (*m e2*)

High-class nightclub across two floors, DJs play good house and techno sounds. *420 Mason Street | tel. 1 415 6 93 07 77 | www.rubyskye.com*

TEN 15 (U E3) (*m e3*)

Megaclub spanning three floors, with a hip laser show into the small hours, often live music. *1015 Folsom Street | tel. 1 415 4 31 12 00 | www.1015.com*

INSIDER TIP ▶ TONGA ROOM (U E2) (*m e2*)

This is the height of kitsch. The pool in the basement of the Fairmont Hotel was redesigned In 1945 with Polynesian grass huts to create the *Tiki Bar* – and has remained so ever since: simply amazing! The dinner menu includes *Hulihuli chicken* accompanied by a Mai Tai or Pina Colada. *950 Mason Street | tel. 1 415 7 72 52 78*

WHERE TO STAY

GREEN TORTOISE HOSTEL
(U F2) (*m f2*)

Mainly young people from all over the world meet at this hostel in North Beach. $40 gets you a dormitory bed, $90 your own double room. *494 Broadway | tel. 1 415 8 34 10 00 | www.greentortoise.com | Budget*

HARBOR COURT HOTEL (U F2) (*m f2*)

Modern-style small hotel only a few steps from the Ferry Building. Some of the ☘ rooms have a view of the Bay. Excellent Japanese in-house restaurant: Ozumo. *131 rooms | 165 Steuart Street | tel. 1 415 8 82 13 00 | www.harborcourthotel.com | Moderate–Expensive*

HOTEL DEL SOL (U D1) (*m d1*)

Charming place in the Marina District; decorated in style and with a great sense of colour. *57 rooms | 3100 Webster Street | tel. 1 415 9 21 55 20 | www.jdv hotels.com | Moderate*

LOEWS REGENCY ☘ (U F2) (*m f2*)

Elegant luxury, international ambience. The winner of several awards with a view of the skyline. *151 rooms | 222 Sansome Street | tel. 1 415 2 76 98 88 | www.man darinoriental.com/sanfrancisco | Expensive*

THE MOSSER HOTEL (U F2) (*m f2*)

Victorian from the outside, modern within. Newly renovated and in a top location between Market Street and SoMa. The lower priced rooms have shared bathrooms. *166 rooms | 54 4th Street | tel. 1 415 9 86 44 00 | www.themosser.com | Budget–Expensive*

ORCHARD GARDEN HOTEL ❀
(U F2) (*m f2*)

Non-toxic wallpaint, the lamps are automatically turned off with the room key – everything has been thought through with a view to its ecological impact. And the location at Union Square is ideal. *86 rooms | 466 Bush Street | tel. 1 415 3 99 98 07 | www.theorchardgardenhotel. com | Expensive*

INFORMATION

VISITOR CENTER (U E–F2) (*m e–f2*)

Brochures, city maps, information and hotel reservations. Salespoint for *Muni* and *City Passes*. *900 Market Street/Powell Street | Hallidie Plaza basement | tel. 1 415 3 91 20 00 | www.sftravel.com*

WHERE TO GO

MUIR WOODS NATIONAL MONUMENT
(132 B–C6) (*m B7*)

Only a good 25 km/15.5 mi north, on Hwy. 101 (exit: Stinson Beach) this nat ural park protects the last of the over 80 m/262.5 ft high *redwoods* of the Bay Area. At the entrance, take an enchanting walk through *Cathedral* and *Bohemian Grove*. In *Mount Tamalpais State Park*, right next to *Muir Woods*, eucalyptus groves break the forest landscape. Two popular surfing beaches lie at the feet of Muir Woods: *Stinson* and *Muir Beach*.

SAUSALITO & TIBURON
(132 C6) (*ID B7*)
Sausalito (pop. 7,300) and Tiburon (pop. 8,300) are two lovable little towns lying opposite San Francisco in Marin County. The nicest thing about both these places are the roads directly on the Bay with their many boutiques, galleries and restaurants. Get a fabulous view of San Francisco Bay from ⚓ restaurants such as *The Trident* and *Spinnaker* or *Barrel House Tavern*. The colourful clutch of 400 houseboats on Richardson Bay north of Sausalito is picturesque.

A particular highlight is the route by ★ ⚓ *Ferry to Sausalito (runs every 1.5 hrs. from the Ferry Building, Journey time: 0.5 h. | Golden Gate Ferry | Market Street/ Embarcadero | tel. 1 415 4 55 20 00)*, which sails straight across the bay past Alcatraz and the Golden Gate Bridge – a perfect brief sightseeing tour.

SILICON VALLEY (134 A2) (*ID B8*)
This neologism for the massive settlement of computer and chip producers in the Santa Clara Valley documents California's power of innovation. However, there's not actually that much to see in terms of high-tech-giants like Intel, Apple or Google. Industrial warehouses, shopping streets and residential areas dominate the scene between Palo Alto and San Jose. Informative and very well done is the *Computer History Museum (Wed–Sun 10am–5pm | admission $17.50 | on the US 101, exit Shoreline Blvd. | www.computerhistory.org)*, whose exhibitions range from old Cray computers to the self-driving Google car.

On the other side of the Bay: Tiburon and Sausalito have become upscale suburbs

THE NORTH

Tough and lonely nature with a rugged coast and an endless forested interior – the over 600 km/373 mi stretch between San Francisco and the border with Oregon is completely different from the sunshine and surf country in the southern part of California.

The sea is cold here, with dangerous currents. But the land of cliffs and fog-shrouded beaches, redwood forests and hidden illegal marijuana plantations offers surprising contrasts. There are active volcanoes with steaming sulphurous springs and charming valleys – one of them the famous Napa Valley – where the best wines of the US are cultivated. It would be a shame to only explore the wine country in a day trip from San Francisco, as Napa only marks the beginning of the north.

EUREKA/ NORTHERN COAST

(132 A–B 1–3) (*A3–5*) **The giant trees growing along the coast, called redwoods or sequoia sempervirens, are amongst the greatest sights in the region** The main settlement is *Eureka* (pop. 26,000) on the wide Humboldt Bay, whose old quarter around Third Street boasts 100 well-preserved Victorian houses from the era of the wealthy lumber barons around 1900. *Fort Humboldt,* at the southern end of town, once served as an observation post to protect the town

The north is sparsely populated,
lovely and wild – a bit like the Wild West
used to be

from Native American attacks. North
of Eureka you'll find some of the most
stunning and lonely beaches in America,
amongst them *North Jetty* at Arcata and
Trinidad State Beach near Trinidad.

SIGHTSEEING

BLUE OX MILL WORKS

This excellent museum village invites
you to travel back in time to the lumber
boom days: with a Victorian-era dock-
yard, a camp and carpentry from 1852
onwards. *Mon–Fri 9am–5pm, Sat 9am–
4pm | admission $10 | 1 X Street | www.
blueoxmill.com*

REDWOOD TREES

Many of the giants with the red
trunks reach nearly 100 m/328 ft into
the sky. *Richardson Grove State Park*
(132 A3) *(⬚ A5)* on Hwy. 101 offers a
charming introduction. A proper parade of them awaits on the shores of
the Eel River, on the ★ *Avenue of the
Giants,* in the *Humboldt Redwoods*

Redwood National Park: Unesco World Natural Heritage since 1980

State Park (132 A–B3) *(⚏ A5)*. For over 50 km/31.1 mi the ☀ panoramic road runs parallel to Hwy. 101.

FOOD & DRINK

SAMOA COOKHOUSE
The last of the old *cookhouses,* where the big *lumber companies* once fed their lumberjacks. Serving calorie-rich rustic fare, the cookhouse doubles up as a museum. *Hwy. 101 across the Samoa Bridge | tel. 1 707 4 42 16 59 | www.samoacookhouse. net | Budget*

LEISURE & SPORTS

HUMBOATS KAYAK ADVENTURES
Kayak hire and guided kayak tours through Humboldt Bay. *601 Startare Drive | tel. 1 707 4 43 51 57 | www.humboats.com*

WHERE TO STAY

CARTER HOUSE INNS
Rooms in splendidly renovated Victorian houses, excellent restaurant. *30 rooms | 301 L Street | Eureka | tel. 1 707 4 44 80 62 | www.carterhouse.com | Moderate–Expensive*

REQUA INN
This historic country inn on Klamath River is perfect as a base for hiking tours into Redwood Country; good food. *15 rooms | 451 Requa Road | Klamath | tel. 1 707 4 82 14 25 | www.requainn.com | Budget–Moderate*

SEA CLIFF MOTEL
Small older motel in an idyllic location in the forest. *4 rooms | 1895 Patrick's Point Drive | Trinidad | tel. 1 707 6 77 34 85 | Budget–Moderate*

INFORMATION

CALIFORNIA'S REDWOOD COAST
322 1st Street | Eureka | tel. 1 800 3 46 34 82 | www.www.redwoods.info, www. nps.gov/redw

WHERE TO GO

FERNDALE ●
(132 A3) *(⚏ A4)*
The sleepy settlement (pop. 1,300) about a half-hour's drive south of Eureka could nearly pass as an architecture museum, considering how many ornate Victorian buildings have been

preserved. The small *Ferndale Museum (closed Mon/Tue)* tells the story of the Eel River valley and the redwood forests. Head for the Ferndale Art and *Cultural Center (580 Main Street)* to admire art by local artists and, in late May, some of the eccentric means of transport employed in the fully ecological INSIDER TIP *Kinetic Grand Championship*: everything is driven by human power only.

THE LOST COAST (132 A3–4) (*A4*)

Here even Highway 1 has to give in. Behind Fort Bragg, the cornice, which dealt with Big Sur so masterfully turns off with a whimper at Leggett to join Hwy. 101. The reason lies straight ahead: a dramatic, deeply jagged coastal landscape. Even the most experienced road builders folded their arms in resignation when they saw this. Scenic highlights are provided by the Sinkyone Wilderness State Park and the King Range National Conservation Area, which you can explore on a hike on the Lost Coast Trail, leading to shipwrecks and an abandoned lighthouse. Information: *Bureau of Land Management (www.blm.gov/ca)*.

REDWOOD NATIONAL PARK (132 A1–2) (*A4*)

Near Orick some 60 km/37.3 mi north of Eureka marks the beginning of the largest protected area for coastal redwoods. Spread over several parcels, the area of around 195 mi² holds some of the world's highest trees – up to 112 m/367 ft high. For a good hundred years the forests were not spared the lumberjacks' axes, until this park was created in 1968. It harbours over 39,500 acres of ancient tree population – just under half of all remaining redwoods. The most beautiful redwood groves with educational trails are situated in the *Prairie Creek Redwoods State Park* along the *Newton P. Drury Scenic Parkway*, in the Lady Bird Johnson Grove and Tall Trees Grove near Orick. The last of these is also the place to pick up free permits for hikes, from the Kuchel Visitor Center on Hwy. 101.

Well worthwhile further north at *Crescent City* is a drive on the Howland Hill Road and the narrow Douglas Park Road through the *Jedediah Smith Redwoods State Park* to *Stout Grove* (no campers). Tip: while the *Trees of Mystery* attraction, complete with a talking Paul Bunyon, the giant of the redwoods, and a cabin lift through the forest at Klamath might be a bit kitschy, it does include a INSIDER TIP Native American museum behind the souvenir shop.

MARCO POLO HIGHLIGHTS

★ Avenue of the Giants
Parade of the huge trees
→ p. 45

★ Lassen Volcanic National Park
Where the earth is still working away → p. 48

★ Mendocino
Colourful artists' villages and surf-beaten cliffs → p. 49

★ Skunk Train
Take the train through redwood forest country → p. 49

★ Mount Shasta
The navel of the world for nature lovers, summit baggers and New Age followers → p. 50

★ Napa Valley
The epitome of Californian wine culture → p. 52

TRINIDAD (132 A2) (𝄞 A4)

The old port a half-hour drive north of Eureka is worth a stop for its magnificent oceanfront location. Other attractions include salmon smokeries such as ⊙ *Katy's Smokehouse (740 Edwards Street)* and good seafood restaurants. Right on a dream-like beach bay, you'll dine like royalty at the *Moonstone Grill (100 Moonstone Beach Road | tel. 1 707 6 77 16 16 | Budget–Moderate)*.

There's a promise of great views nearby at the ● ⋙ INSIDER TIP *Patrick's Point State Park*, one of the most beautiful capes of the northern coast with lonely cliffs, beaches and a reconstructed Yurok Indian village. In spring and autumn you can observe whales from Trinidad.

LASSEN VOLCANIC NAT. PARK

(133 D3) (𝄞 C4–5) ★ **Exposed boulders, cinder cones and bubbling mud and sulphur springs give an impression of what the inside of the last active volcano in California must have looked like.**

There is however no need to be afraid as the nature trails (with a duration of up to several hours) leading to attractions such as the *Sulphur Works Thermal Area* and *Bumpass Hell* are safe

Below the earth it's bubbling, hissing and spitting: Lassen Volcanic National Park

to use and absolutely spectacular. *Hot Rock* is a 400-ton lava boulder, which was thrown through the air for miles. *Chaos Jumbles* consists of hundreds of thousands of pieces of lava debris, scattered across 1.5 mi².

Having been active over 300 times between 1914 and 1921, the volcano is only "sleeping" according to geologists. This National Park can be discovered some 150 km/93 mi southeast of Mount Shasta on Hwy. 89. Mount Lassen is the southernmost summit of the volcanic Cascade Range, 3,178 m/10,427 ft high and covered in snow all year round, although accessible on a hiking route (5 hrs. in the summer).

WHERE TO STAY

BIDWELL HOUSE
Historic villa with charming B & B in a small pioneer settlement on the southern edge of the national park. *14 rooms | 1 Main Street | Chester | tel. 1 530 2 58 33 38 | www.bidwellhouse.com | Budget–Moderate*

INFORMATION

Information on the national park can be picked up from the ranger stations, the largest of which is in the *Loomis Museum* at the northwestern entrance. The *Park Headquarter (SR 36, 14 km/8.7 mi outside the park | tel. 1 530 5 95 44 80 | www.nps.gov/lavo)* is situated in *Mineral*.

MENDOCINO

(132 A4) (⫐ A6) The coast between Gualala and Fort Bragg is dominated by steep cliffs and small wind-swept coves.

Hwy. 1 is dotted with idyllic villages, while further inland you'll find small vineyards. The most famous of the villages is ★ ⚘ *Mendocino* (pop. 800), whose well-preserved Victorian old quarter with its traditional wooden houses has a charming site on a peninsula and is today a centre for arts and crafts.

FOOD & DRINK

CAFÉ BEAUJOLAIS
Gourmet restaurant with a pretty garden. Speciality: sturgeon. Reservations essential. *961 Ukiah Street | tel. 1 707 9 37 56 14 | www.cafebeaujolais.com | Expensive*

GOODLIFE ⚘
An organic bakery also serving breakfast and lunch including gluten-free and vegetarian options. *10483 Lansing Street | Budget–Moderate*

LEISURE & SPORTS

CATCH A CANOE & BICYCLES, TOO!
Hire kayaks, canoes and bikes. A good starting point for nice bike tours along the Pacific coast. *At the Stanford Inn | Ukiah Road/Hwy. 1 | tel. 1 707 9 37 02 73 | www.catchacanoe.com*

SKUNK TRAIN ★
A trip on the historic steam train through the redwood forests from Fort Bragg to Willits is an experience. *Hwy. 1 | Laurel Street | Fort Bragg | tel. 1 707 9 64 63 71 | www.skunktrain.*

WHERE TO STAY

AGATE COVE INN ⚘
Perfect for a honeymoon: small huts in a beautiful location on the coast.

12 rooms. | 11201 Lansing Street | tel. 1 707 9 37 05 51 | www.agatecove.com | Moderate–Expensive

THE ALBION RIVER INN ✷
On the estuary of the Albion River. Some rooms have their own fireplace. ✷ Restaurant with views of the Pacific and good regional food. *22 rooms | 3790 N Hwy. 1 Albion | tel. 1 707 9 37 19 19 | www. albionriverinn.com | Expensive*

MOUNT SHASTA

(132 C1–2) (*Ш B4*) **The region around Mount Shasta and the Cascade range is a country of deep forests, lakes, glaciers and volcanoes, a paradise for hikers, fishermen and canoe enthusiasts.**
In the *Shasta National Forest* you'll find 2,500 km/1,554 mi of lonely hiking trails. The *Shasta Dam* with its 155 m/ 509 ft-high dam retains the water for the artificial *Lake Shasta* with a 500 km/ 311 mi shoreline – a popular area for houseboat tours.

SIGHTSEEING

MOUNT SHASTA ★ ●
At 4,317 m/14,163 ft, the mountain, snow-topped all year round, can be seen from afar, eight glaciers hugging its slopes. Along the way watch out for the steaming hot springs. Once the seat of the Great Spirit for the Indians, Mount Shasta today serves New Age followers as the chosen home of extraterrestrials. The ✷ *Everett Memorial Highway* offers fantastic views of mountains and valleys. From the *Bunny Flat* car park, a trail leads for 8 km/5 mi and up 2,300 m/7,546 ft onto the summit – in a tour only suitable for experienced hikers.

MOUNT SHASTA (TOWN)
A friendly little town (pop. 3,500) at the foot of the mountain of the same name. Many shops here sell crystals and esoteric books. The source of the Sacramento River is a pilgrimage site for Ashram followers and philosophers of nature. Healings and massages are on offer everywhere.

FOOD & DRINK

SEVEN SUNS CAFE
Cosy coffee shop with a patio on the southern edge of town. Only open for breakfast and lunch. *1011 S Mount Shasta Blvd. | Mount Shasta | tel. 1530 9 26 97 01 | Budget*

LEISURE & SPORTS

FISHING
Fishing permits for trout fishing in the Lower Sacramento and other rivers, valid for two or ten days, are available from sports and grocery stores. Tours are ar-

LOW BUDGET

Pancakes or eggs with bacon for breakfast, huge burgers and chunky steaks the rest of the day: Mount Shasta had the first *Black Bear Diner* branch *(401 W Lake Street)*.

A cheap alternative to expensive coastal destinations such as Mendocino, is the former lumberjack settlement of *Fort Bragg* only half an hour's drive further north. Most motel rooms cost under $100 here, one of them the *Surf Motel (1220 S Main Street | tel. 1 800 3 39 53 61)*.

Fly-fishing in the Lower Sacramento River near Redding requires patience

ranged by *The Fly Shop (4140 Churn Creek Road | Redding | tel. 1 800 6 69 34 74).*

HOUSEBOATS

The reservoirs in the Redding area are very popular in the summer for house boat holidays. Booking: *Packer's Bay Marina (Shasta Lake | tel. 1 800 9 59 33 59 | www.shastalake.net);* Lake Trinity: *Trinity Alps Marina (Lewiston | tel. 1 530 2 86 22 82 | www.trinityalpsmarina.com).*

RIVER DANCERS

1 to 3-day rafting trips on the Klamath and Sacramento Rivers. Calm drifting trips for beginners or families – or on raging white water for adrenaline junkies. *705 Kenneth Way | Mount Shasta | tel. 1 530 9 25 02 37 | www.riverdancers.com*

WHERE TO STAY

MCCLOUD HOTEL

Good renovated B & B in a historic building. *4 suites (with jacuzzi), 12 rooms | 408 Main Street | McCloud | tel. 530 9 64 28 22 | www.mccloudhotel.com | Moderate*

MOUNT SHASTA RANCH

An imposing ranch house dating back to 1923 with Bonanza flair. Simply stunning is the ✳ veranda with pretty views of Mount Shasta. *1008 W. A. Barr Road | Mount Shasta | tel. 1 530 9 26 38 70 | www.mountshasta bedandbreakfast.com | Budget–Moderate*

RAILROAD PARK RESORT

Nostalgic, not only for railway fans: in this resort you sleep in restored passenger carriages and brake vans from the Wild West. With pool. *100 Railroad Park Road | Dunsmuir | tel. 1 530 2 35 44 40 | www.rrpark.com | Moderate*

INSIDER TIP ▶ STEWART MINERAL SPRINGS

Hippie nostalgia pure and simple: this idyllically located accommodation has simple chalets, motel apartments, and super-cheap teepees. The cherry on the cake: an old wooden bathing house with a sauna heated by a fireplace. *Weed | tel. 1 530 9 38 22 22 | www.stewartmineral springs.com | Budget*

INFORMATION

SHASTA CASCADE WONDERLAND ASSOCIATION

Welcome Center: *1699 Hwy. 273 | Anderson | tel. 1 530 3 65 75 00 | www.shasta cascade.com*

WHERE TO GO

REDDING (132 C3) (*⌕ B4*)

Good starting point for tours. The attraction of this town (pop. 90,000) just over 100 km/62 mi south is the *Turtle Bay Exploration Park (daily 9am–5pm, Sat/Sun from 10am | admission $16 | Hwy. 44 | www.turtlebay.org).* Extensive gardens with museums and the unique INSIDER TIP *Sundial Bridge,* a cantilever cable-stayed bridge built by Spanish architect Santiago Calatrava across the Sacramento River, also serves as a sundial at the same time.

NAPA VALLEY

(132 C5–6) (*⌕ B7*) ★ **A good 200 vineyards with a cultivated area of 58 mi² cluster in the 40 km/24.9 mi-long wine valley, deservedly the most famous of America.**

The town of Napa (pop. 78,000) at the southern entrance of the valley is the logistical centre, while the cellars are dotted further north along Hwy. 29. If you want to do a round trip, take the Silverado Trail back, on the eastern side of the valley.

SIGHTSEEING

WINE VILLAGES

In the town of *Napa* the recently restored old quarter and the weekly farmer's market *(May–Oct Tue and Sat mornings | 500 First Street) are well worth a visit.* Several excellent restaurants as well as the old distillery *V Marketplace,* today a pretty shopping centre, have made the fame of *Yountville.* Further north, most of the famous vineyards lie around *Rutherford, Oakville and St Helena.* Framed by idyllic hills, *Calistoga* (pop. 5,000) far up north has made a name for itself mainly as a spa, boasting – thanks to the volcanic soil – a true geyser: *Old Faithful.*

VINEYARDS

Most wineries offer tastings *(usually $15–40 charge)* and some also boast first-class restaurants. The minor earthquake in 2014 may have smashed a few bottles, but everything is now back to normal. Good guided tours run at *Beringer*

The fine wines of the Napa Valley are some of the best in the world

Vineyards (*St Helena | tel. 1 707 3 02 75 92*), *Robert Mondavi* (*Oakville | tel. 1 888 766 63 28*) and the *Schramsberg* sparkling wine cellar (*Calistoga | tel. 1 707 9 42 45 58*).

Also worth seeing: *Clos Pegase* with spectacular architecture by Michael Graves (Calistoga), the *Inglenook Winery* of film director Francis Ford Coppola near Rutherford, *Sterling Vineyards* high above the valley near Calistoga as well as the champagne cellar of Domain Chandon (Yountville).

Also of interest is the ⊕ **INSIDER TIP** *Hess Collection* (*tel. 1 707 2 55 11 44 | www.hesscollection.com*) with an exhibition of modern art in the hills above Napa. By the way, Hess was one of the first ten Californian vineyards in 2008 to receive an eco certificate for sustainable wine cultivation without pesticides.

FOOD & DRINK

INSIDER TIP CINDY'S BACKSTREET KITCHEN

California cuisine at reasonable prices. Fabulous wine list, also available to sample in the bar. *1327 Railroad Ave. | St Helena | tel. 1 707 9 63 12 00 | Moderate*

OXBOW PUBLIC MARKET ● ⊕

Gourmet market with organic shops (oysters!), small-scale eateries and several wine sellers. Great organic burgers at Gott's Roadside (*Budget*). *610 First. Street | Napa*

TERRA

Starred restaurant offering California cuisine in perfection. *1345 Railroad Av. | Saint Helena | tel. 1707 9 63 89 31 | Expensive*

ZUZU ⊕

Tasty Spanish-Californian tapas from organic produce and good wines. *829 Main Street | Napa | tel. 1 707 2 24 85 55 | Moderate*

SHOPPING

NAPA PREMIUM OUTLETS

Good outlet with 50 shops of big brands such as Hilfiger, Levi's, Nautica. *Mon–Sat 10am–9pm, Sun 10am–7pm | Hwy. 29 | 1st Street Exit | Napa*

LEISURE & SPORTS

NAPA VALLEY BALLOONS

A unique experience: floating above the vineyards in a hot-air balloon at dawn. *Incl. Champagne brunch approx. $240 | Yountville | tel. 1 707 9 44 02 28*

ST HELENA CYCLERY

Bike hire and route tips. *1156 Main Street | St Helena | tel. 1 707 9 63 77 36 | www.sthelenacyclery.com*

WHERE TO STAY

EL BONITA MOTEL

Stylish nostalgic motel on Hwy. 29 with a garden and pool. *23 rooms | 195 Main Street | St Helena | tel. 1 707 9 63 32 16 | www.elbonita.com | Moderate–Expensive*

INDIAN SPRINGS RESORT & SPA ●

Oldest spa in the spa town of Calistoga, renovated in 2015. Large mineral pool, mudpacks with volcanic ash, massages. *46 rooms | 1712 Lincoln Ave. | Calistoga | tel. 1 707 9 42 49 13 | www.indiansprings calistoga.com | Expensive*

NAPA WINERY INN

Three-storey modern hotel on Hwy. 29 with pool and its own microbrewery. *59 rooms | 1998 Trower Ave. | Napa | tel. 1 707 2 57 72 20 | www.napawineryinn. com | Moderate–Expensive*

NAPA VALLEY WELCOME CENTER
Gives also information about the wineries. *600 Main Street | tel. 1 707 2 51 58 95 | www.visitnapavalley.com*

SONOMA VALLEY

(132 C6) (⌂ B7) The Sonoma Valley is the smaller and less busy of the two famous wine valleys of northern California.
The town Sonoma (pop. 9,600) one hour's drive north of San Francisco on Hwy. 12 is considered the birthplace of Californian wine. Its centre is formed by INSIDER TIP a busy plaza, surrounded by adobe (clay brick) houses, laid out in 1835 by the Mexican general Mariano Vallejo.

East of Glen Ellen you'll find the *Jack London Historic State Park (daily 10am–5pm | admission $10 per vehicle)*, comprising the estate and grave of the writer ("Call of the Wild"). Today, the house is a museum. Right nearby, sample fine Merlot and Sauvignon Blanc in the vineyards of Kunde (9825 Sonoma Hwy.) and Kenwood (9592 Sonoma Hwy.). And just outside the town of Sonoma, the Buena Vista Winery, the oldest vineyard in the region (18000 Old Winery Road, pretty place for a picnic) is also worth a visit. If you've not had enough of vineyards yet, there are numerous other good ones further north around Healdsburg.

FOOD & DRINK

JOHN ASH & CO.
Famous starred restaurant serving California cuisine which stands out through its freshness and variety. There is a small, pretty luxury hotel too (44 rooms). *4350 Barnes Road | Santa Rosa | tel. 1 707 5 27 76 87 | www.vintnersinn.com | Expensive*

INSIDER TIP MAYA
Mexican recipes, cleverly prepared using market-fresh ingredients. *101 E Napa Street | Sonoma | tel. 1 707 9 35 35 00 | Budget–Moderate*

WHERE TO STAY

FAIRMONT SONOMA MISSION INN & SPA
Hotel from the 1920s, where you may enjoy the hot springs – and the spa cuisine that goes with it. *226 rooms | 100 Boyes Blvd. | Sonoma | tel. 1 707 9 38 90 00 | www.fairmont.com | Expensive*

EL PUEBLO INN
Relatively good-value accommodation for the Sonoma region, built in the Hacienda style. *53 rooms | 896 W Napa Street | Sonoma | tel. 1 707 9 96 36 51 | www.elpuebloinn.com | Moderate*

INFORMATION

SONOMA VALLEY VISITORS BUREAU
Maps and information on vineyards, restaurants, etc. *Sonoma Plaza and on Hwy. 121 | Sonoma | tel. 1 707 9 96 10 90 | www.sonomavalley.com*

WHERE TO GO

POINT REYES NATIONAL SEASHORE (132 B6) (⌂ B7)
Lonely beaches, green pastures, jaw-dropping cliffs: Point Reyes is the last great totally unspoilt conservation area on the Californian coast. The dramatic coastal landscapes are an ideal area for hiking, especially in spring when the

wildflowers are in bloom, and you can spot whales – in summer there tends to be a lot of fog. With the conservation area lying just over 50 km/31.1 mi from Sonoma and at the same distance to San Francisco, it's easy to plan a 2 to 3-day round trip taking in the wine country and coast.

Amateur ornithologists will be interested in the Bolinas Lagoon *(www.egret. org)* of the Audubon Canyon Ranch, where in spring hundreds of egrets

SONOMA COAST
(132 B5–6) *(ᗰ A6–7)*

One of the highlights of your California trip awaits between Bodega Bay and Gualala: the Coast with a capital C – steep, jagged and dotted with picturesque coves. The fishing village of Bodega Bay, founded in 1775 and today a bastion of deep-sea fishing, has made cinematic history as the place where Alfred Hitchcock's thriller "The Birds" was filmed. The Fort Ross State Historic Park shelters a reconstruct-

Former country residence of General Mariano Vallejo, founder of the small town of Sonoma

build their nests. Kayak and hiking tours around Tomales Bay and kayak hire can be arranged through *Blue Waters Kayaking (12938 Sir Francis Drake Blvd. | Inverness | tel. 1 415 6 69 26 00 | www. bluewaterskayaking.com)*.

A good place to stay in the valley is the *Point Reyes Seashore Lodge (10021 Hwy. 1 | Olema | tel. 1 415 6 63 90 00 | www. pointreyesseashorelodge.com | Moderate–Expensive)*, which might not be on the ocean, but offers 24 very comfortable rooms.

ed Russian fur trading post from 1812. *Bodega Harbor Inn (14 rooms, 5 cottages | 1345 Bodega Ave. | tel. 1 707 8 75 35 94 | www.bodegaharborinn.com | Budget)* is a comfortable motel a few steps from the water. Further north, near Gualala, lies the more expensive, if more stylish ⊛ *Sea Ranch Lodge (19 rooms | 60 Sea Walk Drive | The Sea Ranch | tel. 1 707 7 85 23 71 | www.searanchlodge.com | Expensive)*, built in the 1960s using a lot of wood in its design, one of the first energy-saving eco resorts in California.

CENTRAL CALIFORNIA

The capital of California? It's neither San Francisco nor Los Angeles, but... Sacramento! The reason that hardly anybody knows this is that the historic centre of the state hides behind its role of fruit and vegetable grower.

It was not far from here however, in the foothills of the Sierra Nevada, that modern California was born. *Gold Country,* reaching from Oakhurst in the south to Nevada City in the north, got its name when, on 24 January 1848, James Marshall discovered the first nuggets while building a sawmill. Soon hundreds of thousands of fortune seekers from all corners of the globe swarmed all over the Sierra Nevada to make their fortune. Some got rich, others found nothing but high prices, wobbly shacks and low-life

bars (there were 50 in the little town of Coulterville alone). Some arrived by ship around Cape Horn, others crossed the continent, where at California's eastern border they still had to overcome the Sierra Nevada, jutting up for over 4,000 m/13,123 ft.

What used to be a bit of light torture is a pleasure today: spectacular pass roads and hiking trails have opened up the dramatic granite world of the High Sierra. Parks such as Yosemite and Sequoia/Kings Canyon or lakes like Lake Tahoe or the bizarre Mono Lake are popular destinations. The most popular region with travellers however, lies further west: the over 650 km/404 mi Pacific coast between San Francisco and Los Angeles. For large stretches this is a landscape that looks

Alpine summits and the road of dreams along the Pacific – contrasts and rich experiences await in the heart of California

as if modern life left it behind, the section between Monterey and San Simeon in particular. Lonely sandy beaches, rugged cliffs and a lot of intact nature accompany Highway 1, the famous road of dreams. This playground of otters, elephant seals and grey whales was immortalised by the impressive images taken by photographers such as Ansel Adams and Edward Weston.

The small towns along the way bear the hallmark of the Spanish, who Christianised the region from Mexico from the mid-18th century onwards. What remains are picturesque mission stations in charming towns such as Carmel, San Luis Obispo and Santa Barbara. Not forgetting the love of cultivating wine, which has been taken up again, and very successfully at that, in the back country of the entire coast.

Whether coming from north or south, the best way to drive the Central Coast is on Hwy. 1, which follows the coast for nearly the entire distance. Just be aware that there are hardly any cross-country connections between the coast and the Sierra Nevada. Which is why the recommended way to do a trip is to first take the coast road down south and then return north along the mountains.

GOLD RUSH TOWNS
In the days of the great gold rush, little towns would often be abandoned as soon

A monument to Claude Chana, a Frenchman who was one of the first gold diggers, in Auburn

GOLD COUNTRY

(133 D–E 4–6) *(Ⓜ C–D 6–8)* **The famous ★ ● Highway 49 runs through the historic Gold Country with its old Western towns along the slopes of the Sierra Nevada from Oakhurst in the south to Nevada City in the north.**

What remains of the great gold rush are the legends immortalised by writers such as Mark Twain, as well as the wooden testimonies scattered across gold diggers' country, of which some are becoming ghost towns, while others have been given the VIP treatment and become shiny museums.

as there were rumours of new finds elsewhere. With its fairly authentic Main Street, the photogenic small Wild West town of **INSIDER TIP** *Jamestown* **(133 E6)** *(Ⓜ C7)* along the southern stretch of Hwy. 49 manages to hold on to the atmosphere of the pioneering days. At the *Railtown 1897 (in summer 9.30am–4.30pm | admission $5 | 5th Ave.)* open-air railway museum you'll recognise many a locomotive from famous Hollywood westerns.

Another settlement that remains well preserved is the old mining town of **INSIDER TIP** *Columbia* **(133 E6)** *(Ⓜ C7)* and *Sutter Creek* **(133 D6)** *(Ⓜ C7)*. 65 km/ 40.4 mi east of Sacramento. The original name for *Placerville* **(133 D5)** *(Ⓜ C6)* was *Hangtown*, because hanging was the most common cause of death here.

The local *El Dorado County Historical Museum (Wed–Sat 10am–4pm, Sun noon–4pm | free admission | 104 Placerville Drive)* gives an insight into the history of Gold Country. At the edge of town, the historic *Gold Bug Mine (in summer 10am–4pm | admission $7 | Bedford Ave.)* has been made accessible once again for visitors, showing the labour-intensive mining life of the time.

North of Placerville, *Coloma (133 D5) (Ⓜ C6)* is the place where James Marshall found that first gold nugget that started everything off. In the *Marshall Gold Discovery State Historic Park* you'll find a reconstruction of *Sutter's Mill*, where Marshall worked.

The old quarter of *Auburn (133 D5) (Ⓜ C6)* (pop. 11,000) is testimony to the wild times of the gold rush. *Empire Mine* near Grass Valley only closed down in 1950, once gold worth 100 million dollars had been extracted from the main shaft. The small town of *Grass Valley (133 D4) (Ⓜ C6)* (pop. 12,000) shelters the *North Star Mining Museum (in summer Tue–Sat noon–4pm | free admission | Allison Ranch Road)*.

In 1850, *Nevada City (133 D4) (Ⓜ C6)* already had 10,000 inhabitants (today, there are only 3,000) and is one of the best-preserved gold-rush towns. Behind the trim façades are antique dealers and good restaurants. 16 km/9.9 mi further north, *Malakoff Diggins Historic State Park (133 D4) (Ⓜ C6)* used to boast the largest gold mine, where the precious metal was washed out of the rocks by hydro power.

FOOD & DRINK

BUTTER CUP PANTRY
Western-style restaurant decorated with numerous relics from the time of the pioneers which is also popular for breakfast. *222 Main Street | Placerville | tel. 0530 6 21 13 20 | Budget–Moderate*

SAINT CHARLES SALOON
A 150 years old and still carrying a whiff of the dodgy. *22801 Main Street | Columbia | tel. 209 5 33 46 56 | Budget*

★ **Highway 49**
Wild West settlements and panoramic views: for over 300 km/186 mi, Highway 49 wends its way through gold prospector country → p. 58

★ **Highway 1**
Perfect dramatic coastal backdrop for your very own road movie → p. 60

★ **Carmel**
Once an artists' colony, today a pretty beach town → p. 62

★ **Monterey Bay Aquarium**
Fascinating underwater world → p. 63

★ **Lake Tahoe**
North America's largest mountain lake → p. 63

★ **Santa Barbara**
A young scene, a happy atmosphere, palm-fringed avenues and fine sandy beaches → p. 68

★ **Sequoia/Kings Canyon**
2,500-year-old giant trees line Generals' Highway → p. 70

★ **Yosemite National Park**
Hiking in one of the most beautiful national parks, famous for waterfalls and sheer rock faces → p. 71

MARCO POLO HIGHLIGHTS

TOFANELLI'S

For breakfast choose from 100 different omelettes, for lunch there are good salads and sandwiches, in the evenings fine steaks. *302 W Main Street | Grass Valley | tel. 1 530 2 72 14 68 | Budget–Moderate*

WHERE TO STAY

1859 HISTORIC NATIONAL HOTEL

Cosy, renovated hotel with saloon and restaurant dating back to the era of the gold diggers. *9 rooms | 18183 Main Street | Jamestown | tel. 209 9 84 34 46 | www.national-hotel.com | Moderate*

HOLBROOKE HOTEL

Once a saloon and brothel, today the best-established accommodation in town. Good restaurant. *28 rooms | 212 Main Street | Grass Valley | tel. 1 530 2 73 13 53 | www.holbrooke.com | Budget–Moderate*

HIGHWAY 1/ BIG SUR

(134 A–B 3–4) (𝄞 B–C 8–9) **For over 150 km/93 mi the ⛰ coastal road winds its way along the dramatic cliffs from Monterey to San Simeon. This is the most beautiful stretch of ★ ● Highway 1, the legendary road along the Pacific.**

It was prisoners who constructed the road in the 1920s. Today the still only two-lane road hugs the cliffs precariously and is sometimes blocked for months after rockslides. Often there's fog right off or on the coast, increasing the atmosphere of wild romance. Back in the day, many famous drop-outs were attracted by the remoteness of this coast. There are few places between the steep rocks where you can access the beach. The most beautiful beaches are INSIDER TIP Pfeiffer Beach *(in Pfeiffer Big Sur State Park | difficult access for large camper vans)*, *Julia Pfeiffer Burns State Park* and *Jade Cove*.

SIGHTSEEING

BIG SUR *(134 A3) (𝄞 B9)*

Many consider this spectacular stretch of coast the heart of Highway 1. This is where 50 years ago the hippie colonies were set up, legendary today. This is where Ansel

LOW BUDGET

Brand-name shirts, shorts, jackets and skirts – the chain store with the lowest prices in California is *Ross – Dress for Less*. Usually, the no-frills shops are situated in shopping malls on the edge of the towns *(e. g. in Pismo Beach: 829 Oak Park Blvd.)*. You'll have to hunt around a bit, but it's well worth the effort.

Any of the better supermarkets will have their own deli section selling sausage, fresh sandwiches, sushi, salads and often also hot dishes such as chicken or spare ribs. Stop for a quick shop, and then take everything to a picnic area to enjoy it with stupendous mountain views.

Discount motels ($50 to $80 per night) are a good alternative for road trips. America's Best Value Inn *(www.americasbestvalueinn.com)* has decent rooms; the modern Motel 6s such as the one in Sacramento are also a good bet. *Motel 6 (tel. 1 415 30th Street | 1916 4 57 07 77 | www.motel6.com)*.

Sandwich stop with a view on Highway 1: Nepenthe terrace restaurant

Adams once took his pictures, and where Henry Miller lived and loved. Hitting Big Sur from the north, an imposing rocky cape with a lighthouse marks its beginning. Extensive coastal panoramas are followed by small redwood forests along the Big Sur River, then, at a Nepenthe, the former summer house of Orson Welles and Rita Hayworth, stunning views open up over the dramatic coast. Tip: only some 400 m/1,312 ft south of the restaurant, on the left hidden behind trees, the **INSIDER TIP** *Henry Miller Library (Wed–Mon 11am–6pm | free admission, donation appreciated)* commemorates the famous writer. Miller's former private secretary, Emil White, established the memorial site, which today also houses art exhibitions, film screenings and readings.

FOOD & DRINK

NEPENTHE ☆

Enjoy burgers and sandwiches atop an 250 m/820 ft cliff with views of the ocean. *48510 Hwy. 1 | just over 5 km/ 3.1 mi south of Big Sur | tel. 1 831 6 67 23 45 | Budget–Moderate*

ROCKY POINT RESTAURANT ☆

Far-reaching views and a pretty terrace on the water some 15 km/9.3 mi south of Carmel. In the winter good for a whale-spotting lunch session. *36700 Hwy. 1 | tel. 1 831 6 24 29 33 | Moderate–Expensive*

WHERE TO STAY

INSIDER TIP **GLEN OAKS BIG SUR** ☺

Stylish motel, ecologically renovated in many aspects, in the valley of the Big Sur River. Very cosy. *17 rooms | Hwy. 1 | Big Sur | tel. 1 831 6 67 21 05 | www.glenoaks bigsur.com | Moderate–Expensive*

NEW CAMALDOLI HERMITAGE ☆

Meditation high above the dramatic coastline? The monks living in this monastery south of Big Sur offer basic single rooms with superb views. *17 rooms | 62485 Hwy. 1 | Big Sur | tel. 1 831 6 67 24 56 | www.contemplation.com | Budget–Moderate (incl. meals)*

MONTEREY PENINSULA

(134 A3) *(🔲 B8)* **At the southern end of this cypress-studded peninsula lies the swathe of land that Robert Louis Stevenson once called "the most beautiful meeting of land and sea on earth": Point Lobos State Reserve.**

On this stretch, the underwater fauna of the Pacific is amongst the most varied in the world – a paradise for hikers and divers. While Point Lobos is fairly unspoilt even on dry land, the Monterey peninsula itself, with its golf links, panoramic drives and well-kept residential colonies, has something of a Californian Côte d'Azur to it.

CARMEL ★

This small town of 4,000 souls, founded as an artists' colony, has become a magnet for tourists, thanks to its magnificent, gently curving bay, many quirky boutiques and fine restaurants.

MONTEREY

One of the earliest settlements founded by the Spanish, who anchored here as early as 1602 and were later to make Monterey (pop. 30,000) the capital of their colony Alta California. Marked in the sidewalk, the Path of History leads to the adobe buildings of the old quarter from the Spanish era. On Fisherman's Wharf, where once the schooners sailing around Cape Horn would come ashore, many restaurants have set

Experiencing whales in their natural habitat is a lifelong dream for many people – the tours begin in Monterey

SEHENSWERTES

17-MILE DRIVE A

Want to see how California's high society lives? Then you're on the right track on this toll road ($10 per vehicle), the panoramic road wending its way from Monterey to Carmel past fine houses and famous golf links such as Pebble Beach.

up shop. There is also the INSIDER TIP Dali17 Museum *(daily 10am–5pm | admission $20 |5 Custum House Plaza)*, which is dedicated to the surrealist who lived there. Cannery Row, once boasting the world's largest canned sardine factory, was immortalised in the novel of the same name by Nobel Prize winner John Steinbeck.

This is also where you'll find the ★ ● Monterey Bay Aquarium *(daily 10am–7pm, in summer 9.30am–6pm | admission $50 | 886 Cannery Row | www.montereybay aquarium.org)*, a particularly fine aquarium: penguins, albatrosses, tuna, sharks and 700 more species of fish are on show. The sea kelp forest across three storeys, the sea otters and jellyfish are also spectacular.

POINT LOBOS STATE RESERVE

With its windswept cliffs, blue bays with frolicking sea otters, and wonderful hiking trails, the conservation area at the southern end of the Monterey peninsula is a true gem of the Californian coastline. At its most beautiful in early morning or at dusk. *On Hwy. 1*

SALINAS

This is the birthplace of John Steinbeck, the chronicler of the Great Depression ("Grapes of Wrath", "East of Eden"). The writer's life and times are documented to great effect in the INSIDERTIP *National Steinbeck Center (daily 10am–5pm | admission $13 | 1 Main Street).*

FOOD & DRINK

KATY'S PLACE

The friendliest breakfast eatery far and wide. *Mission Street/6th Street | Carmel | tel. 1 831 6 24 01 99 | Budget*

MONTRIO ☺

Fresh, local ingredients, fabulous creations and a good wine list. *414 Calle Principal | Monterey | tel. 1 831 6 48 88 80 | Expensive*

LEISURE & SPORTS

KAYAK

An ideal way to come closer to otters, sea lions and dolphins, e.g. with *Monterey Bay Kayaks (693 Del Monte Ave. | Monterey | tel. 1 831 3 73 53 57).*

LAGUNA SECA RANCH GOLF CLUB

Monterey boasts over a dozen golf courses – most of them in private hands. This is one of the few public courses. Due to high demand many clubs charge *green fees* of over $150. Hotels can help with booking tee-off times. *From $40 | Monterey | tel. 1 831 3 73 37 01*

MONTEREY BAY WHALE WATCH

Grey whales may be observed from December through March, blue and humpback whales show up in summer. More tour operators can be found on Fisherman's Wharf. *84 Fisherman's Wharf | tel. 1 831 3 75 46 58 | www.montereybay whalewatch.com)*

WHERE TO STAY

GREEN LANTERN INN

Historical guest house with attractive huts surrounded by greenery not far from the sea. *17 rooms | Casanova Street | Carmel | tel. 1 831 6 24 43 92 | Moderate–Expensive*

INFORMATION

MONTEREY PENINSULA VISITOR AND CONVENTION BUREAU

401 Camino El Estero | Monterey | tel. 1 888 2 21 10 10 | www.seemonterey.com

LAKE TAHOE

(133 E4–5) (⑭ D6) **The extremely clear water of ★ Lake Tahoe remains cool in high summer: not surprising in view of the fact that the largest mountain lake in North America (35 km/21 mi long and 19 km/11.8 mi wide) is situated at 2,000 m/6,562 ft in the Sierra Nevada.**

The surrounding national forests and mountain summits like *Eldorado, Tahoe* and *Toiyabe* rise another 1,200 m/3,937 ft or so above the water level of Lake Tahoe. 274 days of sun in a year and reliable snow conditions make the region a paradise for water sports enthusiasts and skiers. The most famous place for winter sports is *Squaw Valley,* where the 1960 Olympic Winter Games took place.

The area's traditional role as a summer vacation spot was already cultivated by the Washoe Indians. The *Gatekeeper's Log Cabin Museum (in summer Tue–Sun 10am–4pm | admission $3 | 130 W Lake Blvd. | Tahoe City)* has information on this aspect of the country's history. The *Emerald Bay State Park* allows you to enjoy the beauty of the landscape in peace and quiet.

FOOD & DRINK

Dinner in Nevada: it can be worth your while to cross the border. The *Stateline* casinos on the Nevada side of Lake Tahoe offer very good-value buffets – often charging as little as $25–35 for all you can eat! One example is the 🔆 *Forest Buffet* with fabulous views from the 18th storey of *Harrah's.*

INSIDER TIP ERNIE'S COFFEE SHOP
Very popular diner, serving a huge breakfast from 6am and lunch till 2pm. *1207 Hwy. 50 | tel. 1 530 5 41 21 61 | Budget*

WOLFDALE'S 🔆
Californian-Japanese cuisine with a terrace and views of the lake. *640 N Lake Blvd. | Tahoe City | tel. 1 530 5 83 57 00 | Moderate–Expensive*

LEISURE & SPORTS

A relaxed way to enjoy the lake is aboard the paddle steamer Tahoe Queen *(from*

$49 | Ski Run Marina | South Lake Tahoe | tel. 1 800 2 38 24 63). Those who like to combine exploration and exercise should grab a hire canoe, kayak or jetski. *Tahoe City Marina (700 N Lake Blvd. | Tahoe City | tel. 1 530 5 83 10 39).*

WHERE TO STAY

LAKE TAHOE BASECAMP ⊙
Stylish motel renovated with the environment in mind just a few steps from the lake and the lift. *74 rooms | 4143 Cedar Ave. | South Lake Tahoe | tel. 1 530 2 08 01 80 | www.basecamphotels.com | Budget–Moderate*

INFORMATION

LAKE TAHOE VISITORS AUTHORITY
Accommodation, activities, good information on ski holidays and more. *169 Hwy. 50 | Stateline | tel. 1 775 5 88 59 00 | www. visitinglaketahoe.com*

SACRAMENTO

(133 D5) (*ɷ C6–7*) In the days of the pioneers this ranch settlement in the heart of Central Valley was the springboard for the gold fields, which led to it being declared the capital of California in 1854.

Today, the modern city, with 2.3 million inhabitants in the agglomeration around its historic core, is the economic hub of a huge agrarian area. In recent times, Sacramento came to fame as the residence of film star and former bodybuilder Arnold Schwarzenegger, who served as governor of California between 2003 and 2010. Building of his official residence, the *State Capitol* in a city-centre park, begun in 1860. Today it houses historical exhibitions and is open to visitors. Look up: the top of the dome was given a coating of real gold – at the time the state of California, crippled by debt these days, still had plenty of money.

ing items to do with the gold rush. *Tue–Sun 10am–5pm, Thu until 9pm | admission $10 | 216 O Street*

Sacramento's capitol building shines with its historic marble and gold leaf interior

SIGHTSEEING

CALIFORNIA STATE RAILROAD MUSEUM ●

One of America's largest railway museums: over 20 restored locomotives, plus completely furbished carriages including a railway post office and exhibitions on the opening up of the West. Nostalgic steam train trips are available on summer weekends. *Daily 10am–5pm | admission $12 | 2nd Street/I Street | www.csrmf.org*

CROCKER ART MUSEUM

A visit to the oldest museum in the West is worthwhile if only for its pretty old halls. Alongside European, Asian and Californian art, you'll also find interest-

OLD SACRAMENTO

The small old district on the eastern bank of the Sacramento River still exudes some of the flair of the gold-rush era. Old-fashioned shops, museums, historic eateries, the *Old Eagle Theater*, founded in 1849, and over 100 restored buildings. *Between Front and 2nd Street*

SUTTER'S FORT STATE HISTORIC PARK

Reconstructed fort with a fascinating history: around 1840, Johann Sutter from Switzerland established the settlement of "New Helvetia". It was his foreman, Marshall, who discovered the first gold – leaving Sutter empty-handed. There are frequent historic enactments. *Daily 10am–5pm | admission $5 | 2701 L Street*

FOOD & DRINK

33RD STREET BISTRO
Cosmopolitan atmosphere, pretty street terrace, always full. Light fusion cuisine. *3301 Folsom Blvd. | tel. 1 916 4 55 22 33 | Budget–Moderate*

THE FIREHOUSE
Bistro in a former fire station dating back to 1853. Popular for weddings. *1112 2nd Street | tel. 1 916 4 42 47 72 | Expensive*

WHERE TO STAY

THE CITIZEN HOTEL
Retro look of the *Golden Twenties* in a chic newly renovated city hotel near the Capitol. Good restaurant. *198 rooms | 926 J Street | tel. 1 916 4 47 27 00 | www.thecitizenhotel.com | Moderate*

DELTA KING RIVERBOAT
Sleep in style on a restored paddle steamer from the 1920s in Old Sacramento. Lounge, restaurant. *44 rooms | 1000 Front Street | tel. 1 916 4 44 54 64 | www.deltaking.com | Expensive*

INFORMATION

SACRAMENTO VISITORS BUREAU
1002 2nd Street | tel. 1 800 2 92 23 34 | www.visitsacramento.com

SAN LUIS OBISPO

(134 C4) *(∅ C10)* **Lying half-way between San Francisco and Los Angeles, San Luis Obispo (pop. 44,000) is well placed for a stopover, most of all because of the surrounding attractions – the coast with Morro Rock, the wine region of the Edna Valley and the splendiferous Hearst Castle.**

In the heart of the coastal town, the Spanish mission station of *San Luis Obis-*

San Luis Obispo: at the Madonna Inn, no room looks like the next

po de Tolosa was founded by a Spanish Franciscan padre in 1772.

FOOD & DRINK

OLD SAN LUIS BBQ ⊗
Classic southern-style BBQ cooked for hours in a smoker. All organic ingredients and lots of smoky flavour. *670 Higuera Street | tel. 1 805 2 85 24 73 | Budget*

WHERE TO STAY

INSIDER TIP MADONNA INN
The epitome of way-out California: each of the 110 rooms is designed in a different way, one completely made of stone, with a waterfall for a shower, and another one for honeymooners. It's always worth taking a look, and that includes the restaurant. *100 Madonna Road | tel. 1 805 5 43 30 00 | www.madonnainn.com | Moderate–Expensive*

INFORMATION

SAN LUIS OBISPO VISITOR CENTERS
895 Monterey Street | Suite 200 | tel. 1 805 78 12 77 | www.visitslo.com

WHERE TO GO

INSIDER TIP EDNA VALLEY
(134 C4–5) (*Ⓜ C10*)
Over the past few years, the valley immediately south from San Luis Obispo has become the new, not-very-well-kept secret for wine lovers. Via Hwy. 227 you'll reach top-quality estates such as the state-of-the-art *Tolosa Winery (4910 Edna Road | tel. 1 805 7 82 05 00 | www.tolosawinery.com)*, where you can watch proceedings from the tasting room. Other good cellars include *Edna Valley Vineyard (2585 Biddle Ranch Road | tel. 1 805 5 44 58 55)*

and ⬇ *Baileyana Winery (5828 Orcutt Road | tel. 1 805 2 69 82 00)*, residing in a former school with views across the valley and a pretty picnic area.

HEARST CASTLE (134 B4) (*Ⓜ C9*)
Near San Simeon, some 70 km/43.5 mi north of San Luis Obispo, you can see the gilded turrets and red-tiled roofs of *Hearst Castle* from far away. Built by newspaper baron William Randolph Hearst, who borrowed from various different European architectural styles, the castle welcomes 1 million visitors a year. This fantasy world cost the publisher 3 million dollars and 30 years (1917–47). His life inspired Orson Welles to make the classic film "Citizen Kane". The 100 rooms in the *Casa Grande*, the pools and the many small houses, where Hearst hosted all Hollywood and famous politicians, give an idea of the luxury life of the time. *Guided tours $25–36 (reservations recommended in summer) | tel. 1 800 4 44 44 45 | www.hearstcastle.org*

MONTANA DE ORO STATE PARK & MORRO ROCK (134 B4) (*Ⓜ C10*)
Some 20 km/12.4 mi north of San Luis Obispo, La Canada de Los Osos is the gateway to Montana de Oro, one of the most beautiful state parks in California, boasting lonely sandy beaches, jagged cliffs, eucalyptus forests and fields of wildflowers – a paradise for hikers, swimmers and campers.
North of Los Osos, Morro Rock is a gigantic volcanic rock, which served the Spanish explorers as orientation and is today a conservation area for falcons. On the opposite side of the bay, amidst white sand dunes, you can find out more about the history of this landscape in the Morro Bay State Park with its Museum of Natural History.

SANTA BARBARA

(135 D6) *(🛵 D11)* ⭐ Santa Barbara has the heartbeat of the Californian Riviera: marinas, palm-fringed avenues, flowering gardens and a young scene thanks to the university on the northern edge of town.

Santa Barbara (pop. 92,000) was founded in 1786 by the Spanish, and their architectural influence and flair still pervade the town today. Marked by red stones on the sidewalk, the *Red Tile Tour* leads to the buildings from the Spanish era *(start at the County Courthouse, Anacapa Street).*

SIGHTSEEING

MISSION SANTA BARBARA

In 1820, Franciscan padres established what is arguably the most beautiful mission in California, complete with a façade inspired by a Roman temple. Destroyed by an earthquake in 1925, it has since been restored to its original state. *Daily 9am–4.15pm | admission $9 | Upper Laguna Street*

FOOD & DRINK

CRUSHCAKES & CAFE

A runaway success: cupcakes. Alongside the sweet retro treats, the café serves a good breakfast and lunch. *1315 Anacapa Street | tel. 1 805 9 63 37 52 | Budget*

ENDLESS SUMMER 🍴

Good drinks accompany fresh fish and steaks from the grill. The pretty view across the marina is free. *113 Harbor Way | tel. 1 805 5 64 12 00 | Budget–Moderate*

THE LARK ⊘

Rustic dining room with the feeling of a summer house. The food served is modern Californian style, ecologically conscious and made with local ingredients wherever possible. *131 Anacapa Street | tel. 1 805 2 84 03 70 | Expensive*

SHOPPING

At the end of State Street, right on the sea, *Stearns Wharf* has shops and restaurants. Every Sunday, *Palm Park* hosts the INSIDER TIP *Santa Barbara Arts and Crafts Show*, where artists sell their handiwork. You are invited to a shopping stroll in *El Paseo (Canyon Perdido Street | between State and Anacapa Street),* where the Spanish occupiers were once trading.

BEACHES

West and east of the city, discover over 50 km/31.1 mi of fabulous sandy beaches popular for windsurfing, swimming, diving and sailing.

WHERE TO STAY

BRISAS DEL MAR

Old Spanish, but renovated and relatively close to the beach. *31 rooms | 223 Castillo Street | tel. 1 805 9 66 22 19 | Moderate*

FOUR SEASONS BILTMORE

An old, restored grand hotel with tropical gardens, tennis courts, pools and a putting green. *207 rooms | 1260 Channel Drive | tel. 1 805 9 69 22 61 | www.fourseasons.com/santabarbara | Expensive*

INFORMATION

SANTA BARBARA VISITORS CENTER

1 Garden Street | tel. 1 805 9 65 30 21 | www.santabarbaraca.com

WHERE TO GO

CHANNEL ISLANDS NATIONAL PARK
(134–135 C–D6) (*C–D11*)
Five of the uninhabited islands off the coast between Santa Barbara and Ven-

SANTA YNEZ VALLEY (134 C5) (*D11*)
Half-an-hour's drive inland from Santa Barbara takes you to the landscape around Hwy. 154 that was made famous by the movie "Sideways": idyllic vineyards, lush pastures and stud farms. A

Shops in Spanish colonial style: the Paseo Nuevo in Santa Barbara

tura shelter sea-lion colonies, rare brown pelicans and many other indigenous species. The sea around the islands also belongs to the park and harbours unique underwater kelp forests. Boat tours from Santa Barbara, as well as spectacular ● diving tours can be arranged through *Truth Aquatics (301 W Cabrillo Blvd. | tel. 1 805 9 62 11 27 | www.truthaquatics.com)*; Whale and dolphin-watching boat trips are offered by *Condor Express (301 W Cabrillo Blvd. |tel. 1 805 8 82 00 88 | condorexpress.com)*.

fun place to visit at the northern end of the valley is *Solvang,* a Danish folk village with half-timbered houses. Good for wine tastings: *Firestone Vineyard (5017 Zaca Station Road)* or the ◎ *Sunstone Winery (125 Refugio Road | Santa Ynez)* which uses purely ecological methods. In Buellton, you get great steaks at INSIDER TIP *AJ Spurs (350 E Hwy. 246 | tel. 1 805 6 86 16 55 | Moderate)*.
For accommodation try *Solvang Gardens Lodge (24 rooms | 293 Alisal Road Solvang | tel. 1 805 6 88 44 04 | www. solvanggardens.com | Moderate)*.

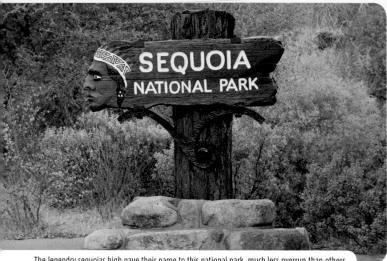

The legendry sequoias high gave their name to this national park, much less overrun than others

SEQUOIA/ KINGS CANYON

(135 D–E 2–3) *(⚏ E8–9)* ⭐ **The two interconnected national parks Sequoia and Kings Canyon are less touristy than Yosemite National Park. They are home to Mount Whitney, at 4,418 m/14,495 ft the highest peak of the Lower 48, and also the world's highest trees, towering sequoias.**

SIGHTSEEING

GIANT TREES
The largest of them all, the General Sherman Tree in the Giant Forest, is 2,500 years old, has a circumference of 34 m/111.5 ft and reaches 90 m/ 295.3 ft, i.e. the height of a 27-storey building. The General Grant Tree in Grant Grove reaches 88 m/288.7 ft and has a circumference of 35 m/114.8 ft. More impressive even than these individual trees are the many other giant trees that you can admire at each side of the Generals' Highway and the hiking trails starting from it. Anyone not keen on walking along the trails can explore *Grant Grove* on horseback just like the first pioneers – an especially impressive way to expreience these massive trees. Book at *Grant Grove Stables (tel. 1 559 3 35 92 92).*

WHERE TO STAY

WUKSACHI LODGE ✪
The most recent hotel in the park has won an award for its ecological construction. The lodge also runs a comfortable campsite for hikers, Bearpaw Camp, around 15 km/9.3 mi inland from the mountains. *102 rooms | 64740 Wuksachi Way | tel. 866 8 07 35 98 | www.visitsequoia.com | Moderate*

INFORMATION

KINGS CANYON VISITOR CENTER

Starting point for hikes, e.g. 3 km/1.9 mi along the Big Stump Trail, documenting the earlier logging of the giant trees. *Grant Grove | tel. 559 5 65 33 41 | www. nps.gov/seki*

YOSEMITE NATIONAL PARK

(134–135 C–D1) (*[]] D7–8)* **Boasting nearly 4 million visitors each year, ★ Yosemite National Park counts amongst America's most popular attractions.**

Situated in the high alpine heart of the Sierra Nevada, the park protects over 1,158 mi² of varied habitats, reaching from the forested foothills of the Sierra to snow-capped peaks. 80 types of mammals, black bears and mountain lions amongst them, as well as over 250 different bird species live here.

Established by Congress in 1890 at the behest of legendary environmentalist John Muir (1838–1914) in order to save the unique mountain habitat in this sector from logging, the park today is crisscrossed by over 420 km/261 mi of roads and a network of hiking trails three times as long. Like other famous parks, Yosemite National Park is also in danger of being destroyed by the masses of visitors it receives. A few decades ago, traffic jams and trampled meadows were an everyday occurrence. Since then, the rangers have been taking countermeasures: tourists are now asked to leave their cars and use the shuttle buses provided. Also, many of the sensitive alpine meadows are barred to visitors for the time being.

SIGHTSEEING

INSIDER TIP GLACIER POINT ☼

From the rocky brow of a hill lying 1,000 m/3,281 ft above the valley bottom, the view sweeps across mountaintops, waterfalls and the backcountry of the High Sierra, devoid of human habitation. Later on, stargazers come out in force: the night sky above Glacier Point is a feast for the eyes! *Only June–Oct, side road from Hwy. 41*

MARIPOSA GROVE

At the southern tip of the park, some 500 sequoias escaped the lumberjacks' attentions. 80 m/262.5 ft high and up 3,000 years old, they turn the grove into a shady cathedral. After extensive renaturation, the grove is open for visitors. A shuttle service runs from the southern entrance of the park to the hiking trails that lead to Grizzly Giant and the Upper Grove.

TIOGA PASS ●

North of the Yosemite Valley, Hwy. 120 wends its way up into the *High Sierra*. This is a country of emerald-green lakes, rock domes and alpine meadows. The most pretty of them all, *Tuolumne Meadows,* is the starting point for beautiful hikes into backcountry. Some of the trails north of Highway 120 cross through areas, which were hit by forest fires and still recover. Leave the park via the *Tioga Pass* at 3,031 m/9,944 ft, forming its eastern entrance. *Only open mid-May–Oct*

YOSEMITE VALLEY ☼

Just under 11 km/6.8 mi long, this valley on the Merced River forms the heart of the park. Receiving 95 per cent of all park visitors, it is chronically full in the summer, partly because of the hotels, restaurants and campsites. Hwy. 140 leads through the Arch Rock Entrance

Yosemite National Park: spectacular landscape with roaring waterfalls

monolith is the symbol of the park and can be climbed on the John Muir Trail (just under 27 km/16.8 mi) on a demanding day walk. Enjoy a view of all attractions at once from the a Wawona Tunnel View Point on Hwy. 41.

FOOD & DRINK

THE MAJESTIC YOSEMITE HOTEL ☆
Like a fortress, the log cabin of a silver-mine baron built from granite and pine logs in the spectacular landscape. Particular recommended: steak, lamb and trout. *Yosemite Village | tel. 209 3 72 14 89 | Moderate*

IRON DOOR SALOON
The oldest saloon in California hosts live music every weekend. *18761 Main Street | Groveland | tel. 1 209 9 62 89 04 | Budget*

INSIDER TIP ▶ YOSEMITE BUG CAFÉ ◎
Cosy café with an organic focus at the western entrance of the park. Popular among hikers and climbers for a tasty breakfast or a hearty steak dinner after a visit to the park. The adjacent hostel offers double rooms and rustic tents. *6979 Hwy. 140 | Midpines | tel. 1 209 9 66 66 66 | www.yosemitebug.com | Budget–Moderate*

WHERE TO STAY

In the park itself, beside the historic *Majestic Yosemite Hotel,* the more basic *Yosemite Lodge Aramark (tel. 1 602 2 78 88 88 | www.travelyosemite.com)*

HOTEL CHARLOTTE
Basic rooms in a rustic old gold-prospector's lodge. Holiday apartments too. *13 rooms | 18736 Main Street | Groveland | tel. 209 9 62 64 55 | www.hotelcharlotte. com | Moderate*

Station into the valley, 20 minutes away, where an unforgettable panorama opens up: hollowed out by glaciers into a massive U, sheer granite walls tower up to 1,000 m/3,281 ft above the valley. All around are waterfalls, wildflower meadows and pine forests. Short trails lead to the attractions.

The 190 m/623 ft *Bridal Veil Falls* and the 739 m/2,425 ft *Yosemite Falls* provide popular photo opportunities. Impossible to miss and a mecca for climbers: El Capitán, a monumental, 1,077 m/3,533 ft block of granite. The eastern end of the valley is dominated by the Half Dome. Up to 3,000 m/9,843 ft high, this naked

INFORMATION

Visitor centres can be found in the *Yosemite Valley* and at *Tuolumne Meadows* near the eastern entrance. *tel. 1 209 3 72 02 00 | www.nps.gov/yose, www. yosemite.com*

WHERE TO GO

BODIE ● (133 F6) *(ᄴ E7)*

Thanks to its remote location on the eastern slopes of the Sierra Nevada, a two-hour drive from Tioga Pass in Yosemite, Bodie embodies the ideal of a ghost town. 150 houses are preserved much as they were left. Even the dirty dishes are still on the table. In 1859 William Bodey hit silver here. Fortune-hunters soon followed, and 20 years later, 10,000 people were living here and working to exhaustion in 30 mines. Nobody lives here anymore, and for the past 50 years nothing has been allowed to change in the little town, now known as Bodie State Historic Park – a dream for amateur photographers (access via US 395 and SR 270). There is no accommodation in the park, but if you feel like spending the night in style in gold-rush ambience, your best bet is the Bridgeport Inn *(8 rooms | Main Street | Bridgeport | tel. 1 760 9 32 73 80 | www.thebridgeportinn.com | Budget)*, where Mark Twain once laid his head, with restaurant, pub and a big dab of pioneer nostalgia.

MAMMOTH (135 D1) *(ᄴ E7)*

This modern resort (pop. 7,000) around one hour's drive east of Yosemite Park is known mainly for its perfect ski pistes on Mammoth Mountain. In summer, the most popular activities here on the dry sunny eastern slopes of the Sierra Nevada are hiking and mountain biking. The massive basalt pillars of the Devils Postpile National Monument on the edge of town are worth seeing.

MONO LAKE (133 F6) *(ᄴ E7)*

At a good 20 km/12.4 mi in diameter, the lake immediately east of Yosemite, and at least 760,000 years old, is California's largest salt lake. While the lake's ecosystem feeds millions of migratory birds, the use of its water to benefit far-away Los Angeles has been threatening it for decades. The fight of environmentalists against this, and the bizarre tuffstone pillars (best seen on its southern banks) have turned the lake into an icon of environmental protection. At the moment water levels are rising again. The information centre of the *Mono Lake Committee (www.monolake.org)* on the main road in Lee Vining documents the fight for the conservation of the lake.

WOODEN RECORDS

The mammoth trees in California are the broadest trees in the world and the redwoods also the highest. But that is not all: the oldest trees in the world, Bristlecone pines, also grow in California These trees can be as much as an amazing 5,000 years old – unbelievable, but true! These ancient trees can be found beyond Yosemite Park near Bishop in the White Mountains growing at an altitude of over 3,000 m/ 9,843 ft. Mountain air must be really healthy.

LOS ANGELES

◈◈ MAP ON PAGE 138/139

◈◈ If this is your first time in Los Angeles (136 B4–5) (Ⓜ E11), you might well be confused. L.A. is not your regular metropolis in the traditional sense of the word, but a mega-city (13.5 million inhabitants), a colourful quilt of districts and individual cities covering about 4,633 mi².

However, this vital counterpoint to New York and by now, thanks to its fabulous museums, cultural centre of the West Coast does have focal points. The wealthy towns along the 65 km/40.4 mi of coast, such as Malibu, Pacific Palisades, Santa Monica, Venice Beach and Marina del Rey, are part of the package. But Downtown too, which due to the fear of earthquakes only got its skyscrapers very late, is experiencing a construction boom of spectacular architecture such as *Disney Hall*. Or take the palm-crowned residential quarters of the stars in Beverly Hills and the hills of Hollywood. Last but not least there are slums in East and South Central Los Angeles with their fair share of race riots and war between trigger-happy youth gangs.

On the freeways, eight to ten-lane motorways, Angelenos spend an average of four hours of the day in traffic jams. The infamous smog has cleared significantly in recent years, but on hot days without a breeze from the sea an unhealthy haze still hovers over the city. With distances being what they are, you can't really do without a car. Do study the map thoroughly before setting off, and avoid rush hour.

Relaxed into the traffic jam:
the sprawling mega-city still exerts
a magnetic attraction

CITY WHERE TO START?

For the best L.A. feeling take a stroll along the promenade of **Santa Monica (138 A4)** *(⎈ E11)* *(multi-storey car park: Broadway/4th Street)*, which officially doesn't even form part of L.A. The nearby Palisades Park runs along the cliffs above the Pacific. By bike, car or bus (blue lines 1 and 2) carry on to Venice for L.A.'s craziest beach.

An interesting cross section of the city can be experienced on a drive down Sunset Boulevard. Starting from Chinatown and the poorer neighbourhoods around Downtown, the famous road leads west. First up is the time-honoured movie capital of Hollywood and the young, quirky West Hollywood, followed by chic Beverly Hills and finally Bel Air, with the villas of the super-rich, before the road ends at the Pacific, where a good number of film stars have settled in Malibu.

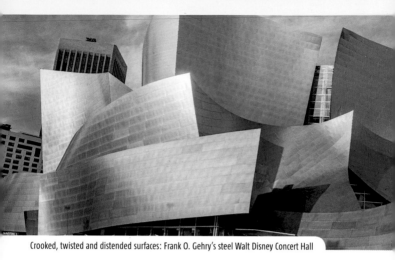

Crooked, twisted and distended surfaces: Frank O. Gehry's steel Walt Disney Concert Hall

SIGHTSEEING

ACADEMY MUSEUM (138 C3) (*E11*)
A museum devoted to the history of the Oscars is long overdue: now it is being built! The planned opening date is in 2019. *Wilshire Blvd./ Fairfax Av. | www.oscars.org*

AUTRY NATIONAL CENTER / MUSEUM OF THE AMERICAN WEST (139 D1) (*E11*)
Wild West art and collectors' items such as Buffalo Bill's saddle. Video screens show old westerns. *Tue–Fri 10am–4pm, Sat/Sun 10am–5pm | admission $14 | Griffith Park I-5/Fwy. 134 | www.theautry.org*

INSIDER TIP BERGAMOT STATION ARTS CENTER (138 A4) (*E11*)
Around 30 galleries exhibit avant-garde art and objects created by contemporary Californian artists in a former factory site. While exploring the area, you can for example discover Andy Warhol's works in the *Revolver Gallery*, the *Skidmore Contemporary Gallery* which specialises in modern painting, the *Robert Berman Gallery* which frequently exhibits photography and videos and also a *Gallery Cafe*. *Open Tue–Fri 10am–6pm and Sat 11am–5.30pm | Admission 15$ | 2525 Michigan Av. | www.bergamotstation.com*

BEVERLY HILLS (138 B–C3) (*E11*)
In a place where so many of the rich and famous live – whether Diana Ross, Jack Nicholson, Sylvester Stallone, Jennifer Lawrence, Bruce Willis, Warren Beatty or Jay Leno – city maps with their addresses (star maps) are a runaway success. The folders are sold by ambulant vendors along Sunset Boulevard. You can explore the most interesting addresses on a drive (going on foot reveals you instantly as a tourist), "discovering" garden walls, gardeners and manicured hedges, as well as the police patrols of Beverly Hills.
On and around Rodeo Drive between Bedford and Rexford Drive, Santa Monica and Wilshire Boulevard, lies the ★ Golden Triangle. This is where you'll find the world's most expensive shops and some 130 restaurants for a break in style.

This complex honeycomb structure is home to the art museum *The Broad (Tue/Wed 11am–5pm, Thu/Fri 11am–8pm, Sat 10am–8pm, Sun 10am–6pm | free admission | 221 S Grand Ave.)*

Union Station, the railway station of Los Angeles *(800 N Alameda Street),* is worth a detour for the design of its waiting room in the Moorish style – a backdrop often seen in Hollywood movies. From here, the *Coast Starlight* can take you to Oakland and San Francisco.

City Hall (200 N Spring Street) is one of the city's tallest building. With its predominantly Spanish-speaking clientele, the INSIDER TIP Grand Central Market (317 S Broadway) is the most vibrant in town. The time-honoured Biltmore Hotel (506 S Grand Ave./W Fifth Street) offers tea in the lobby, designed in Old Spanish style – a place still suggestive of the lustre of times past. A simple and fast way to get around the downtown area of under

Another attraction are famous hotels such as the Beverly Wilshire (9500 Wilshire Blvd.), where Richard Gere found movie happiness with his Pretty Woman.

DOWNTOWN (139 E3–4) (*ω E11*)

The city centre lies south of the crossing of two main traffic arteries, the Hollywood and the Harbor Freeway. This is the only collection of high-rise buildings in the entire flat area of the city as effectively confirmed by the view from the Observation Platform of the *US Bank Tower (633 W Fifth Street).* Here you will also find the latest attraction in L.A. to get your adrenalin going: a glass slide descending over 310 m/1,017 ft. Sweaty palms guaranteed!

Alongside banks and office towers, Downtown is most of all a centre for the arts. Don't miss the Music Center, on the slopes right next to the Opera, and the Walt Disney Concert Hall (111 S Grand Ave./1st Street), de-signed in 2003 by Frank Gehry in his typically flowing forms. A new 140 million dollar cultural building opened its doors right next door in 2015.

MARCO POLO HIGHLIGHTS

★ **Golden Triangle**
Luxury shops and fine restaurants around Rodeo Drive → p. 76

★ **Getty Center**
Enjoy great art in ultra-modern architecture → p. 78

★ **TCL Chinese Theatre**
Stars and starlets on Hollywood Boulevard → p. 78

★ **Universal Studios Hollywood**
A round trip through the stage sets of the movie world → p. 80

★ **Venice Beach**
Colourful epicentre of Californian beach culture → p. 80

a square mile is the Dash minibus service (50 cents). Its F route leads to the Staples Center, a sports and entertainment complex on the southern end of Downtown, where the Grammys are staged.

GETTY CENTER ★ ● ☼
(138 A3) (*𝄞 E11*)
The world's richest museum, boasting an endowment of 2 billion dollars, resides in an ultramodern complex by New York architect Richard Meier high above Brentwood. The splendid view across the seemingly endless urban landscape of L.A. makes a visit worth while. The collections put together by oil magnate Jean Paul Getty include mainly highlights of European art before 1900. *Tue–Sun 10am–5.30pm, Sat until 9pm | free admis-sion, parking fee $15 | 1200 Sepulveda Blvd. | access via I-405*
The large antiques collection of the museum is housed in the famous Getty Villa by the sea. *Wed–Mon 10am–5pm | free admission (online pre-booking recommended), parking fee $15 | 17985 Pacific Coast Hwy. | www.getty.edu*

GRAMMY MUSEUM (139 E3) (*𝄞 E11*)
The city's nicest attraction for music fans: four floors of interactive exhibitions on the winners and plenty of music to take a listen. *Daily 11.30am–7.30pm, Sat/Sun from 10am | admission $13 | 800 W Olympic Blvd. | www.grammymuseum.org*

HOLLYWOOD BOULEVARD
(138 C2) (*𝄞 E11*)
What remains from the glory days of the old studios you'll find on Hollywood Boulevard between Vine Street and La Brea Avenue, where – nearly hidden by the shops selling souvenirs and T-shirts – there's the ★ TCL Chinese Theater (6925 Hollywood Blvd.). The courtyard of the dragon-festooned, pagoda-style cinema is the place where in 1927 Mary Pickford and Douglas Fairbanks started the tradition of leaving prints of their hands and feet in the fresh cement. Today, over 200 Hollywood greats are immortalised on the pavement. TCL still sometimes stages a prestigious evening film premiere where stars and paparazzi come out in force. Opposite, further magnificent cinemas from Hollywood's heyday await, such as the El Capitan Theatre or the Egyptian Theatre, where once "Ben Hur" and "My Fair Lady" celebrated their first night.
Most film stars however may be spotted each year at the Oscar ceremony next door at the Dolby Theatre *(guided tours daily 10.30am–4pm | $23 | 6801 Hollywood Blvd./Highland Ave.)*, a snazzy entertainment complex with shops and restaurants. Around it, the sidewalks on Hollywood Boulevard boast the Walk of Fame, pink marble stars with the names of show business VIPs. Since 1960, over

LOW BUDGET

L. A. might not exactly be famous for its public transport system, but you'll be surprised at all the places the *Metro Day Pass ($7, $25 for a week)* will get you to.

● Always wanted to be on TV? In L.A. this is no problem – even if it's only as a part of the audience for television shows such as the "Tonight Show" or "Jeopardy". Free tickets: *www.tvtix.com* or *www.tvtickets.com*

For discounts on admission fees, tours and restaurants check the website *www.discoverlosangeles.com* under deals.

2,500 stars' names have been embedded into the pavement – these days, for 10,000 dollars each, as the stars have to pay to be immortalised. From the a terraces to the rear of the Hollywood & Highland Center you can see the famous Hollywood sign, designed in huge white letters, in the hills above the city.

holds one of the INSIDER TIP▶ biggest cactus plantations in the world as well as a Chinese garden. There is also British art from the 18th and 19th centuries in the Art Gallery. *Wed–Mon 10am–5pm | admission $23, at weekends $25 | 1151 Oxford Road | San Marino | www.huntington.org*

The stars shine brightly on the Walk of Fame on Hollywood Boulevard

INSIDER TIP THE HOLLYWOOD MUSEUM ● (138 C2) (*Ø E11*)

Across four floors, this museum tells the story of the film industry with the aid of old posters, original costumes and stage sets. The make-up rooms of legendary makeup artist Max Factor, the former owner of the building, is particularly beautiful. *Wed–Sun 10am–5pm | admission $15 | 1660 N Highland Ave. | Hollywood | www.thehollywoodmuseum.com*

HUNTINGTON LIBRARY, ART COLLECTIONS & BOTANICAL GARDENS (136 B4) (*Ø E12*)

L.A. superlatives: the library holds six million books and manuscripts, amongst them a Gutenberg Bible. And the square mile of botanical gardens

LOS ANGELES COUNTY MUSEUM OF ART (LACMA) (138 C3) (*Ø E11*)

The 130,000 artworks making up the treasures of the biggest museum in the western United States include European and American art, but also exceptional Korean and Japanese works. The most striking new building within this large complex is the *Broad Museum of Contemporary Art at LACMA* created by Renzo Piano at a cost of 150 m/492 ft dollars which frequently houses gigantic-dimensioned installations. *Mon/Tue, Thu 11am–5pm, Fri 11am–8pm, Sat/Sun 10am–7pm | admission $15 | 5905 Wilshire Blvd. | www.lacma.org*

MUSEUM OF CONTEMPORARY ART (MOCA) (139 E3) (*Ø E11*)

Eye-catching building by Arato Isozaki. Inside, Pop Art and changing shows

Venice Beach is a great place to explore on two wheels

await. For more avant-garde art, including some great works and installations, head for the adjacent Geffen Contemporary (152 N Central Ave./First Street). *Wed–Mon 11am–6pm, Thu until 8pm, Sat/Sun until 5pm | admission $15 | 250 S Grand Ave. | www.moca.org*

SANTA MONICA (138 A4) (*∅ E11*)
L.A.'s beach suburb has turned into a centre of the creative avant-garde. There's a cluster of galleries and new restaurants on Main Street, and in the afternoons and evenings, the pedestrianised Third Street Promenade becomes one of the most popular promenades in the whole of Los Angeles.

Only a few more steps further on, pretty, leafy a Palisades Park stretches along Ocean Avenue. Stroll on the cliffs above the beach, framed by palm trees and agave blossoms, and enjoy the views of the Pacific and the Santa Monica Mountains. On Santa Monica Pier at the end of Colorado Avenue you'll find plenty of T-shirts for sale, souvenirs and a merry-go-round for the smallest visitors.

UNIVERSAL STUDIOS HOLLYWOOD ★
(138 C2) (*∅ E11*)
The guided tour around the film studios where series such as "Columbo" and films like "Terminator," "Pirates of the Caribbean – The Curse of the Black Pearl" or "Indiana Jones" were made, offers a glimpse of backstage life. Add to this rollercoasters, stunt shows, movie attractions like *Transformers* or *The Simpsons*, who live in a reconstructed Springfield, and an in-house nightlife area, Universal City Walk.

True highlights are the *Waterworld* stunt show and and the new *Wizarding World of Harry Potter* that opened in 2016, where fans will surely recognize many figures and scenes from the films. Demand is accordingly high, which is why you should schedule the studio tour right at the beginning of your visit. *Daily 10am–6pm, in summer 9am–8pm | admission $105–116 | Freeway 101/3900 Lankershim Blvd. | www.universalstudioshollywood.com*

VENICE BEACH ★ ● (138 A5) (*∅ E11*)
On the weekend, the Boardwalk, the slightly run-down promenade and an emblem of Californian fitness culture, awakens to new life. Venice Beach is still a meeting place for musclemen on their bodybuilding training regime, while on the Boardwalk bikini-clad in-line-skater girls and bronzed cyclists show off their bodies and skills. Cafés,

bike and skate hire outfits and souvenir stalls cluster at the foot of Windward Avenue, where you can also watch in-line-skate artists perform in a bike park. Discover quirky restaurants, galleries and trendy shops on a stroll along INSIDER TIP Abbot Kinney Blvd. only a few streets further inland.

TOURS

L. A. CONSERVANCY
Each Saturday, the teaching staff of this architectural association lead groups through the historic centre, to the grand old cinema palaces on Broadway and the modern design buildings of Downtown. Various departure points. *$10 | tel. 213 6 23 24 89 | www.laconservancy.org*

STARLINE TOURS
Half or whole day tours through Hollywood to the villas of the VIPs in Beverly Hills and Malibu. *Pickup from hotel. tel. 323 4 63 33 33 | www.starlinetours.com*

FOOD & DRINK

CAFÉ DEL REY ⊻ (138 B5) *(ﾉ E11)*
Light California cuisine with Mediterranean touches. Plenty of fresh fish and free views of the marina. A well known meeting point for singles where they mix powerful drinks. *4451 Admiralty Way | Marina Del Rey | tel. 1 310 8 23 63 95 | Expensive*

COLD STONE CREAMERY (138 E5) *(ﾉ E11)*
Tasty, freshly-made ice cream is scooped up behind the counters of this food chain, e.g. at *36 Washington Blvd. | Marina del Rey | Budget*

GEOFFREY'S/MALIBU ⊻ (136 A4) *(ﾉ E11)*
Popular destination for brunch or lunch on a cliff on the Pacific coast. *27400 Pacific Coast Hwy. | north of Malibu Canyon | tel. 1 310 4 57 15 19 | Moderate*

HAMA SUSHI (138 A5) *(ﾉ E11)*
Casual Japanese restaurant under a tent roof with a surfing flair and creative Sushi. *213 Windward Av. | Venice Beach | tel. 1 310 3 96 87 83 | Moderate*

HILLSTONE (138 A4) *(ﾉ E11)*
Smart restaurant with outdoor seating, modern Californian dishes, Sushi and a good wine list. *202 Wilshire Blvd. | Santa Monica | tel. 1 310 5 76 75 58 | Moderate*

STAGE-SET CITY L.A.

Do you sometimes get this strange feeling of "I've been here before"? Small wonder, as Hollywood producers find the best sets right outside their front door – with good weather thrown in for free. The beaches of Santa Monica, the streets of Westwood and Beverly Hills – they've all served as backdrops for thrillers, soaps and cult classics. It was at the Beverly Wilshire Hotel that Richard Gere fell in love with Julia Roberts *(Pretty Woman)*, Brad Pitt was strolling through Downtown with Angelina Jolie as *Mr. and Mrs. Smith*, and *Superman* flew over the tower of City Hall. So keep your eyes peeled when you see large trucks, trailers and spotlights: filming is taking place!

LALA'S GRILL (138 C3) (*Ø E11*)
A young crowd plus lots of energy come with sangria, Argentinian steaks and other South American delights served on the lovely terrace. *7229 Melrose Av. | Hollywood | tel. 1323 9 34 68 38 | Moderate–Expensive*

LEMONADE ◎ (138 A4) (*Ø E11*)
Healthy, fresh, tasty and quick service – is this all possible at once? Yes, in the branches of this chic fast-food chain, fine dishes and vegan food are served in cafeteria style. *301 Arizona Av. | Santa Monica | Budget*

M STREET KITCHEN (138 A4) (*Ø E11*)
Young, trendy restaurant plating up excellent fish tacos, burgers, Japanese Sushi and southern-style fried chicken. *2000 Main Street | Santa Monica | tel. 1 310 3 96 91 45 | mstreetkitchen.com | Moderate*

INSIDER TIP MEL'S DRIVE-IN
(138 C2) (*Ø E11*)
A coffee shop straight out of a movie – frequented by many stars, by the way. To get into the mood, check out the website: www.melsdrive-in.com. *8585 Sunset Blvd. | West Hollywood | Budget*

PINK'S HOT DOGS (138 C3) (*Ø E11*)
America's best hot dogs served until 2am! It is a great place to get to know some locals as you wait to order. *709 N La Brea Ave./Melrose Ave. | Hollywood | Budget*

REPUBLIQUE (138 C3) (*Ø E11*)
The former film studio of Charlie Chaplin has been turned into a courtyard with balconies in which the stars meet to dine rather than to act. *624 S La Brea Av./Wilshire Blvd. | West Hollywood | tel. 1 310 3 62 61 15 | Moderate–Expensive*

INSIDER TIP URTH CAFFÉ ◎
(138 A4) (*Ø E11*)
Cosy coffee house serving organic coffee and good desserts. *2327 Main Street | Santa Monica | tel. 1 310 3 14 70 40 | Budget*

SHOPPING

Large malls are everywhere in L.A., some of them proper palaces of shopping such as the Beverly Center (138 C3) (*Ø E11*) (8500 Beverly Blvd./Third Street) with fancy US brand stores and restaurants such as the Hard Rock Café sporting a bright green Cadillac on its roof. The large Santa Monica Place Mall has a true Californian feel and a lovely terrace restaurant on the upper floor (138 A4) (*Ø E11*) (315 395 Santa Monica Place).

There are also good shopping opportunities on Sunset Strip (138 C2) (*Ø E11*), more specifically on the 8600 block of Sunset Blvd., on Montana Avenue (house numbers 900–1400), popular with many actors too, and on Main Street (138 A4) (*Ø E11*) in Santa Monica.

L. A. FARMER'S MARKET
(138 C3) (*Ø E11*)
Market stalls with a large selection of groceries; the adjacent shopping centre The Grove sells designer clothing. The restaurants and snack bars here are often frequented by stars working out of the neighbouring CBS TV studio. *Mon–Fri 9am–9pm, Sat until 8pm, Sun 10am–7pm | 6333 W 3rd Street/Fairfax Ave. | West Hollywood*

MELROSE AVENUE (138 C3) (*Ø E11*)
Many unusual shops, plus sandwich shops and cappuccino bars in low-rise restored houses from the 1920s, often complemented by conspicuous façades. With their European-inspired retro look, the boutiques set the fashion tone for all

America. *Shops usually 11am–8pm | between Fairfax and La Brea Ave. | West Hollywood*

SANTA MONICA FARMER'S MARKET ⊗ (138 A4) *(Ⓜ E11)*
Saturday is organic market day. On Sundays bands play too, while eco-conscious restaurants take turns to display their culinary prowess. *Sat 8am–1pm (3rd Street/ Arizona Ave.), Sun 8.30am–1.30pm (2640 Main Street) | Santa Monica*

SPORTS & BEACHES

GOLD'S GYM (138 A4) *(Ⓜ E11)*
The most famous bodybuilding studio in the entire States. *360 Hampton Drive | Venice | tel. 1 310 3 92 60 04 | www.goldsgym.com*

BEACHES
☀ Santa Monica Beach with its splendid panorama is the beach that is the easiest to reach from the city centre. Continuing north, you'll find the beaches Surfrider, Malibu Lagoon, Point Dume, Zuma Beach County Park and Leo Carillo, which are also popular with surfers. Southwards, Venice Municipal, Playa del Rey, Redondo State Beach and Manhattan Beach, headquarters for the beach volleyball players, who stage tournaments here, await.

ENTERTAINMENT

For events listings, see the daily newspaper Los Angeles Times as well as the free LA Weekly *(www.laweekly.com)*.

PLAYHOUSE (138 C2) *(Ⓜ E11)*
Top nightclub that stretches over several floors. Features international DJs on Fridays and Saturdays. It's best to register ahead via the website. *6506 Hollywood Blvd. | Hollywood | tel. 1323 6 56 48 00 | playhousenightclub.com*

ROXY ON SUNSET (138 C2) *(Ⓜ E11)*
Live stage with excellent daily changing bands of any musical creed. *9009 W Sunset Blvd. | West Hollywood | tel. 1 310 2 78 94 57 | www.theroxy.com*

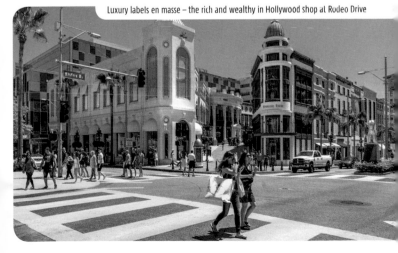
Luxury labels en masse – the rich and wealthy in Hollywood shop at Rodeo Drive

SADDLE RANCH (138 C2) (*♨ E11*)
Have you ever tried riding on a mechanical bull? Now is the time to try it out in this Wild West party location in the nightlife district. *Sunset Blvd. | West Hollywood | www.thesaddleranch.com*

THE VIPER ROOM (138 C2) (*♨ E11*)
Live performances and bar; this well-known club used to belong to Johnny Depp – and was the place where River Phoenix collapsed and died. Many celebrities come here, but there's a ban on taking pictures! *8852 Sunset Blvd. | West Hollywood | tel. 1 310 3 58 18 81 | www.viperroom.com*

WEST END (138 A4) (*♨ E11*)
Depending on which DJ is working the decks, there's a whole musical kaleidoscope of hip-hop, salsa, funky sounds and reggae. Salsa night every Monday. *1301 5th Street | Santa Monica | www.wendendsm.com*

WHERE TO STAY

Keep in mind that L.A. is huge. The best places for a base are Santa Monica/Venice, Westwood, West Hollywood and Beverly Hills.

INSIDER TIP **ACE HOTEL**
(139 E3) (*♨ E11*)
This small, ultra-stylish hotel in a splendidly renovated United Artists' cinema in downtown L.A. brings the era of silent films back to life. *182 rooms | 929 S Broadway | tel. 1 213 6 23 32 33 | www.acehotel.com | Expensive*

CAL MAR SUITES (138 A4) (*♨ E11*)
Respectable motel with 36 large suite-rooms and a good location towards the seaside. *220 California Ave. | Santa Monica | tel. 1 310 3 95 55 55 | www.calmarhotel.com | Moderate*

CARLYLE INN (138 C3) (*♨ E11*)
Basic, but quirkily styled house on the edge of Beverly Hills. *32 rooms | 1119 S Robertson Blvd. | tel. 1 310 2 75 44 45 | www.carlyleinn.com | Moderate*

HOTEL ERWIN (138 A4) (*♨ E11*)
Hip design hotel right on Venice Beach. Very trendy: the open-air lounge on the a rooftop terrace. *119 rooms | 1697 Pacific Ave. | Venice Beach | tel. 1 310 4 52 11 11 | www.hotelerwin.com | Moderate*

HILGARD HOUSE (138 B3) (*♨ E11*)
Cosy hotel in Westwood. Shops, restaurants and university within walking distance. *55 rooms | 927 Hilgard Ave. | tel. 1 310 2 08 39 45 | www.hilgardhouse.com | Moderate*

MONDRIAN (138 C2) (*♨ E11*)
Still the coolest hip accommodation in West Hollywood – created by world-famous French designer Philippe Starck. Lobby, pool and the *Sky Bar* (reservations essential) are hang-outs for the stars. In-house restaurant *Ivory on Sunset. 238 suites | 8440 Sunset Blvd. | Olive Street | West Hollywood | tel. 323 6 50 89 99 | www.mondrianhotel.com | Expensive*

SEA SHORE MOTEL (138 A4) (*♨ E11*)
Friendly motel, right in the thick of the action of Venice and within walking distance of the beach. 19 rooms | *2637 Main Street | Santa Monica | tel. 1 310 3 92 27 87 | www.seashoremotel.com | Budget–Moderate*

VENICE BEACH COTEL (138 B4) (*♨ E11*)
Backpacker hostel right on Venice Beach; basic dorm rooms but also private doubles. *40 beds | 25 Windward Ave. | tel. 1 310 3 99 76 49 | www.venicebeachcotel.com | Budget*

A quick island trip from Los Angeles? Santa Catalina Island is only a one-hour ferry ride away

INFORMATION

BEVERLY HILLS VISITOR CENTER
(138 B3) *(𝄞 E11)*
9400 S Santa Monica Blvd. | tel. 1800
3 45 22 10 | www.lovebeverlyhills.com

LOS ANGELES VISITORS INFORMATION
CENTER (139 E3) *(𝄞 E11)*
6801 Hollywood Blvd. | tel. 1323 467
64 12 | www.discoverlosangeles.com

SANTA MONICA VISITOR
INFORMATION CENTER
(138 A4) *(𝄞 E11)*
Palisades Park | 1400 Ocean Av. | tel. 1310
3 93 75 93 | www.santamonica.com

WHERE TO GO

PASADENA (136 B4) *(𝄞 E11)*
Not even 15 km/9.3 mi northeast of L.A.,
Pasadena (pop. 140,000) boasts an old
quarter, which around Colorado Avenue
has become a meeting place. The *Norton*

Simon Museum (139 F1) *(𝄞 E11)* *(Mon,
Wed/Thu noon–5pm, Fri/Sat 11am–
8pm, Sun 11 am–5pm | admission $ 12
| 411 W Colorado Blvd.)* shows drawings
by Picasso and works by Kandinsky and
Klee, with pretty gardens thrown in.
The city is also a mecca for antique deal-
ers, who cluster on Holly Street between
Fair Oaks and Los Robles. Every second
Sunday of the month, the Rose Bowl
Flea Market is held at the football sta-
dium, one of the biggest in the US with
2,500 vendors.

SANTA CATALINA ISLAND
(136 B5) *(𝄞 E12)*
The island (pop. 4,000), its beaches empty during the week, is situated about
30 km/18.6 mi from L.A. and can be ac-
cessed by ferry from Long Beach and San
Pedro (return ticket approx. $80 per per-
son). Chewing gum baron William Wrig-
ley built the casino in the island capital
of Avalon, and his villa is a luxury hotel
today. *www.catalinachamber.com*

THE SOUTH

If you're travelling along the west coast, a beach holiday really only makes sense south of Los Angeles. Here, the water of the Pacific is warm enough to support the colourful, crazy beach life of surfers and beach volleyball glorified in countless films.

Southern California covers a large area though, dishing up many contrasts. You'll experience the region's civilised face along over 150 km/93 mi of coast. Here, the population has downright exploded over the past decades: from L.A. to the Mexican border, there's one house after another, and one shopping mall after another. Given an easy air through the artificial fun of the entertainment parks, enhanced by museums for contemporary art, crisscrossed

by straight-as-a-die roads and endowed with pretty beaches, this region doesn't wear its history on its sleeve. It's easy to forget that it was 20 km/12.4 mi north of San Diego that the first European landed in California in 1542, in the shape of the Portuguese explorer Juan Rodriguez Cabrillo.

The built-up coastal region is however only one face of southern California. Beyond the coastal mountains another, much lonelier world awaits: the desert realm that makes up about a quarter of the entire state.

Biologists divide the region into the hot, forbidding Colorado Desert in the south and the slightly cooler, higher Mojave Desert with its characteristic yucca palms further north. Today, large sections of the

Photo: The high desert ecosystem of the Mojave Desert

Discover the Golden State's sunny south: pretty beaches, a hot desert and the easy life

deserts enjoy protection as state and national parks such as Death Valley or Joshua Tree. But the American armed forces have also marked parts of the empty landscapes for their own use: as test areas or landing places for space shuttles at the Edwards Air Force Base. And then there are oases like Palm Springs – the gilded desert city. Residing between green golf courses and swimming pools in palm-fringed estates of this luxurious resort, rich and prominent Californians spend their winters.

ANAHEIM

(136 B4–5) (*D F11*) **Anaheim would have been only one of the many southern suburbs of Los Angeles – if it hadn't been for Walt Disney's arrival in 1955.**
This is where he realised his life's dream: a theme park offering more than just rollercoasters and merry-go-rounds. Since then, the city has grown rapidly (350,000 inhabitants today) and turned fun into big business.

ANAHEIM

SIGHTSEEING

DISNEYLAND ⭐

The world's oldest entertainment park. However, state-of-the-art high-tech rollercoasters such as Indiana Jones or the 3-D attraction Star Tours make sure that the park stays up to date. However, older attractions in the park, divided up into different lands, are worth seeing: the boat trip through the fantasy world of the Pirates of the Caribbean for instance, or the Jungle Cruise.

Younger children tend to prefer the actors in Mickey and Goofy costumes as well as Snow White and other well-known fairytale figures. *In summer usually daily 8am–10pm | admission $97–124, good-*

Disneyland: the Matterhorn in the Magic Kingdom

value tickets valid over several days available too | I-5 Exit Disneyland Drive | tel. 1 714 7 81 45 65 | www.disneyland.com

DISNEY'S CALIFORNIA ADVENTURE

The second Disney park in Anaheim is right next to Disneyland – not quite as large, but more modern and California-themed. Particularly good fun are the Muppet Show and the breathtaking California Screamin' roller-coaster. *Variable opening times, in summer usually daily 10am–8pm | prices and combined tickets as Disneyland*

WHERE TO STAY

DISNEYLAND HOTEL

With its own play and entertainment facilities, connected with Disneyland by Monorail train. *969 rooms | 1150 Magic Way | tel. 1 714 7 78 66 00 | www.disneyland.com | Expensive*

MARRIOTT RESIDENCE INN

Modern hotel with 200 humungous suites. Suitable for families. *11931 Harbor Blvd. | tel. 1 714 5 91 40 00 | www.residenceinnanaheim.com | Moderate*

SUPER 8

One of the many motels within walking distance from Disneyland and some 10 km/6.2 mi from Knott's Berry Farm. *173 rooms | 415 W Katella Ave. | tel. 1 714 7 78 69 00 | www.super8anaheim.com | Budget*

WHERE TO GO

CHRIST CATHEDRAL (136 B5) (𝄞 F11)

Daring ecclesiastical construction by a TV preacher made from over 10,000 glass panels. The building has been used by the Catholic church since 2013. *Guided tours Mon–Sat 10am and 1pm | 12141 Lewis Street | Garden Grove | 9.65 km/6 mi from Anaheim*

INSIDER TIP KNOTT'S BERRY FARM
(136 B4–5) (*M F11*)

Only a 15-minute drive further west another huge entertainment park awaits, a must-do for fans of rollercoasters. The most exciting rides are the 30-storey *Supreme Scream* and *Silver Bullet*. There are also whitewater rides, a Wild West ghost town, and for kids *Camp Snoopy*. You want to cool down? Look out for the connected, gigantic water park, *Soak City USA*, right next door. *In summer usually 10am–10pm, at other times closing earlier in the evening | admission $75 | 8039 Beach Blvd. | Buena Park | www.knotts.com*

QUEEN MARY (136 B5) (*M E11*)

The British luxury liner, once the world's largest passenger ship, today lies at anchor in the harbour of Long Beach, approx. 40 km/24.9 mi from Anaheim, serving as a museum and hotel. Open to the public are the captain's bridge, the engine room and the upper decks. *Daily 10am–6pm | admission from $28–34 | 1126 Queens Hwy. | Long Beach | www.queenmary.com*

COLORADO RIVER AREA

(137 F3–5) (*M H10–11*) **Dammed into several large lakes, the Colorado River – the greatest and most important river in the American Southwest – forms the border between California and Arizona.** In recent times, the desert region on both banks of the river has developed into a playground for Californians: with large marinas, many campsites and casinos on the Nevada side.

SIGHTSEEING

TOWNS ON THE COLORADO

Needles (137 F3) (*M H10*) is a small town with many historic buildings from the days of the Santa Fe Railroad and beautiful campsites along the river. In *Lake Havasu City* (137 F4) (*M H11*), millionaire Robert P. McCulloch had the old *London Bridge*, taken apart on the banks of the Thames in the early 1970s, rebuilt

MARCO POLO HIGHLIGHTS

★ **Disneyland**
Walt Disney's first entertainment park in Anaheim set the benchmark for leisure parks all over the world, and continues to do so → p. 88

★ **Death Valley**
Endless desert sand, salt lakes and rocks sporting all colours – a magical valley full of extremes → p. 90

★ **Laguna Beach**
Pretty coastal town with plenty of art and tradition – and a wonderful beach bay → p. 92

★ **Joshua Tree National Park**
Bizarre rocks and tree-high yuccas in the heart of the Mojave desert → p. 95

★ **San Diego Zoo**
One of the world's best zoos: enclosures mimicking natural environments, a staggering variety of species, with over 4,000 animals, and guided tours by bus → p. 96

★ **Sea World**
In this huge leisure park, sea lions, orcas, polar bears and penguins take centre stage → p. 96

Lake Havasu: a recreational lake that also supplies water to Los Angeles and San Diego

stone by stone. *Blythe* (137 F5) *(⑳ H11)* is the starting point for a trip on the Colorado – by canoe or raft.

Half-day and full-day canoe and rafting tours into the gorges of the Colorado and boat hire are available from *Jerkwater Canoe Company (Topock | Arizona | tel. 1 800 4 21 78 03 | www.jerk watercanoe.com)*. For general information on the region contact the *Needles Chamber of Commerce (Front Street and G Street | tel. 1 760 3 26 20 50 | www. needleschamber.com)*.

DEATH VALLEY

(136–137 C–D 1–2) *(⑳ F–G 8–9)* **Rocky wasteland and extreme flimmering heat have a name in California: Death Valley. Badwater, the lowest point of the USA, is located in ★ ● Death Valley, too.**
Framed by peaks reaching heights of up to 3,368 m/11,050 ft, like ⤴ *Telescope Peak*, and filled with saltwater lakes, nowhere does the diversity of desert life become clearer than along the 180 km/112 mi of the "valley of death". Huge craters, remnants of former volcanoes, and striking canyons shine in dazzling multicolour, thanks to metal and mineral deposits, and shelter a bizarre variety of shapes. *Furnace Creek* forms the centre of the national park, with motels, campsites, restaurants, a public swimming pool and interesting exhibitions at the *Visitor Center*.

SIGHTSEEING

ARTIST'S PALETTE DRIVE
This side road of US 178 leads to a rock formation which looks its best when the morning and evening light brings out the colours of a painter's palette. The slanted light of the sun also serves to illuminate the large sand dunes at *Stovepipe Wells* to best effect. As far back as the 1920s, Hollywood filmed the first "Arab" desert movies here.

SCOTTY'S CASTLE
This is the unfinished dream of adventurer Walter Scott, who in 1924 with the

help of a Chicago businessman erected a Moorish-inspired castle in a lonely canyon for 2.4 million dollars. *123 Scotty's Catle Road*

ZABRISKIE POINT/DANTE'S VIEW ☀

The *Zabriskie Point* viewpoint high above the eroded hills and dried-up lakes of the desert was made famous by Michelangelo Antonioni's film of the same name. At least as impressive however – in the early hours of the morning in particular – is the view from *Dante's View,* spanning the entire length of the valley.

WHERE TO STAY

FURNACE CREEK RANCH & INN

An extensive oasis with motel rooms and rustic ranch huts near the lowest point of the valley – and the lowest golf course in the world. Slightly removed, on the slopes, lies the historic *Inn,* open only between October and May, where many Hollywood stars have spent the night. *Ranch 224 rooms, Inn 66 rooms |*

Furnace Creek | tel. 1 760 7 86 23 45 | www.furnacecreekresort.com | Moderate–Expensive

INFORMATION

FURNACE CREEK VISITOR CENTER

190 California Highway | Furnace Creek | tel. 1 760 7 86 32 00 | www.nps.gov/deva

WHERE TO GO

MOJAVE NATIONAL PRESERVE
(137 D–E 2–3) (*M G–H10*)

The Americans call the Mojave Desert some 80 km/49.7 mi further south, High Desert, as it lies at an altitude between 1,000 m/3,28 ft and 1,600 m/5,249 ft. Animals (coyotes, tortoises, hares) and plants (cacti, other types of succulents, mesquite trees) thrive in great numbers. In the spring, the wildflowers (the most pretty being the Californian poppy) turn many sections into a sea of colours.

Cima Dome is a 500 m/1,640 ft granite monolith, which has Joshua trees grow-

THE THREAT OF THE DESERT

Alicia Sanchez embarked on an excursion to Death Valley at the beginning of August 2009. She was found a few days later by chance, by a park ranger in a state of partial dehydration on a side road with her jeep buried up to the axles in sand. The real tragedy was that her eleven-year-old son had not survived the heat and lack of water. Alicia came from Las Vegas. One could imagine that she was familiar with desert conditions, but somewhere she had made a wrong turning, misunderstood the GPS and did not have sufficient

water with her. It is a case like this that the otherwise so fascinating and seemingly harmless desert can swiftly become life-threatening; similar events occur again and again in the southwest of the USA. These can however be avoided by adhering to a few rules: take 5 l water per person and day with you and have more petrol in your tank than you need for the entire route. Never camp in dry river beds – if it rains in the hinterland, floods can occur without warning. Another useful tip: have tweezers ready to pull out cactus spines ...

ing on its surface. Cinder Cones National Natural Landmark shelters conical volcanic craters and prehistoric rock paintings.

LAGUNA BEACH

(136 B5) *(Ⓜ F12)* **With its pretty cliff location, this beach town has an interesting tradition, even if, with 23,000 inhabitants,** ⭐ **Laguna Beach has long expanded beyond the borders of the original artists' colony.**
Art and crafts still play an important role, in summer in particular, when between July and late August the large-scale *Festival of Arts* takes place in *Irvine Bowl Park*.

SIGHTSEEING

LAGUNA ART MUSEUM
Large and fine exhibitions of both modern and older southern Californian artists. *Thu 11am–9pm, Fri–Tue 11 am–5pm | admission $7 | 307 Cliff Drive*

FOOD & DRINK

LAS BRISAS ⚜
Buzzing Mexican place serving tacos and margaritas – under the open sky with a view of the ocean. *361 Cliff Drive | tel. 1 949 4 97 54 34 | Expensive*

ZINC CAFÉ & MARKET ☻
Airy café for breakfast and lunch with a gourmet market attached. From Wednesday to Sunday they serve dinner too. Not specifically advertising itself as organic, yet all ingredients are regional and super-fresh. *350 Ocean Ave. | tel. 1 949 4 94 63 02 | Moderate*

WHERE TO STAY

ART HOTEL LAGUNA BEACH
Basic, oldish motel with a pool, not far from the beach. *28 rooms | 1404 Coast*

Drinking plenty of water is essential at temperatures of over 35 °C/95 °F in the desert

Kelso Dunes and Devil's Playground are fascinating sand dune landscapes. Amongst the most beautiful routes are Kelbaker Road (the north-south connection between Baker and the I-40) and Mojave Road, the old Indian trail, drivable by jeep (hire one in Las Vegas or Palm Springs). *Information: Kelso Depot Information Center (Kelso | tel. 1 760 2 52 61 08 | www.nps.gov/moja)*

Hwy. | tel. 1 949 4 94 64 64 | www.artho tellagunabeach.com | Budget–Moderate

INN AT LAGUNA BEACH ⚓

Well-kept beach hotel, designed with a lot of taste with airy California feeling. *70 rooms | 211 N Coast Hwy. | tel. 1 949 4 97 97 22 | www.innatlagunabeach.com | Expensive*

RITZ-CARLTON LAGUNA NIGUEL ⚓

Considered one of the 20 best hotels in the US. It certainly enjoys a beautiful location above the rocks right on the sea, with two swimming pools, a spa and three restaurants. *396 rooms | 1 Ritz Carlton Drive | Dana Point | tel. 1 949 2 40 20 00 | www.ritzcarlton.com | Expensive*

INFORMATION

LAGUNA BEACH VISITORS BUREAU
381 Forest Av. | tel. 1 949 4 97 92 29 | www.visitlagunabeach.com

WHERE TO GO

DANA POINT (136 B5) *(ш F12)*

Ideal for a walk after visiting the beach: numerous restaurants and shops are congregated around the old harbour area of this town (pop. 36,000) just under 10 km/6.2 mi south of Laguna Beach. Day tours to *Santa Catalina Island* depart from this location.

HUNTINGTON BEACH ●
(136 B5) *(ш E12)*

Here you can almost imagine the Beach Boys singing "Surfing USA". This is no surprise as the town (pop. 200,000) just under 20 km/12.42 mi north of Laguna Beach has been the most legendary surfing location in California for almost a century. You can watch the surfers from

above on the long pier. On Main Street, the names of legendary surfers from all round the world are cast in bronze tiles on the *Surfing Walk of Fame*. The surf crowd are accordingly out in force here, especially for the championships in early September. The small *International Surfing Museum (Tue–Sun noon–5pm | admission $2 | 411 Olive Ave.)* celebrates the masters of the art. A lot more upmarket is the next town along, Newport Beach (136 B5) *(ш F12)*, (pop. 80,000) with fancy galleries and shops on Fashion Island. Nearly 10,000 yachts can fit into the harbour – giving rise to the nickname "American Riviera". The excellent Orange County Museum of Art *(Wed–Sun 11am–5pm, Thu until 8pm | admission $12 | 850 San Clemente Drive)* mainly shows provocative contemporary art.

SAN JUAN CAPISTRANO
(136 C5) *(ш F12)*

Some 15 km/9.3 mi from Laguna Beach in the hills, this historic town (pop. 36,000) full of colonial-style adobe buildings around the ruins of the Spanish INSIDER TIP *Mission San Juan Capistrano (daily 9am–5pm | admission $9 | Hwy. 74)* founded in 1776, with an excellent museum and the oldest church in California, takes its name from the Italian crusader preacher John of Capistrano (14–15th centuries).

PALM SPRINGS

(137 D5) *(ш G11)* **Hot springs have always been the attraction of the Coachella Valley near Palm Springs (pop. 46,000), a spa resort beyond the coastal mountains of Los Angeles, now trendy once more.**

On the northern edge of the town, the turbines of big wind farms cover the desert country. The electricity gained is urgently needed for water pumps and cooling plants. Today, the *Coachella Valley* has around 125 golf courses, 300 tennis courts and way over 7,000 pools.

To this day, the Cahuilla Indians in the *Agua Caliente Indian Reservation* own most of the land. Through income from leasing it out they are amongst the richest tribes in the US. In the *Indian Canyons,* 8 km/5 mi south of the centre of Palm Springs city, you can go for beautiful rambles along the brook through wild palm groves *(in summer only open at weekends).* East of Palm Springs, on East Palm Canyon Drive, you'll see a string of oases of the good life. *Rancho Mirage, Indian Wells, Palm Desert* – all refuges of wealthy early retirees who spend their days golfing and their evenings sipping martinis on the terrace.

SIGHTSEEING

INSIDER TIP THE LIVING DESERT

Desert lovers will have a great time here: the open-air enclosure of 1.8 mi² is home to hundreds of cacti, plus snakes, mountain sheep and many other desert animals in their natural habitat. The adjoining 🌀 *Palo Verde Garden Center* sells ecologically grown cacti and other desert plants – ideal souvenirs. *Daily 9am–5pm, in summer 8am–1.30pm | admission $20 | 47-900 Portola Ave. | Palm Desert | www.livingdesert.org*

PALM SPRINGS AERIAL TRAMWAY 🏂

This cable car takes hardly 20 minutes to swing from the desert floor over 4 km/2.5 mi to a height of 2,640 m/8,661 ft above sea level. On a clear day, you can see for up to 130 km/81 mi from the last stop! In the *San Jacinto State Park*

(136 C5) (Ⓜ F11) you'll find cool pine forests, 80 km/49.7 mi of hiking trails and – in snowy winters – pistes for cross-country skiing as well as ski hire outlets. *Mon–Fri 10am–8pm, Sat/Sun 8am–8pm | admission $26, our tip: after 4pm, the price for the cable car incl. dinner goes down to only $36 | Hwy. 111*

PALM SPRINGS ART MUSEUM

The emphasis here is on modern American and Indian art. *Sat–Tue 10am–5pm, Thu/Fri noon–9pm | admission $15 | 101 Museum Drive*

FOOD & DRINK

BLUE COYOTE GRILL

A popular grill: The spicy specialities from the southwest are worth the wait. *445 N Palm Canyon Drive | tel. 1 760 3 27 11 96 | Moderate*

SHOPPING

DESERT HILLS PREMIUM OUTLETS

A huge shopping centre on the northern edge of the Coachella Valley with 130 discount shops of top brands like Armani and Versace. *Mon–Sat 10am–9pm, Sun 10am–8pm | Freeway I-10 Cabazon*

WHERE TO STAY

COYOTE INN

Nice small hotel in the adobe style, rooms with kitchen, pool. *7 rooms | 234 S Patencio Road | tel. 1 760 3 27 03 04 | www.coyoteinn.net | Moderate–Expensive*

PALM MOUNTAIN RESORT

Simple middle-class hotel with a pool in an ideal location at the centre of town. *118 rooms | 155 S Belardo Road | tel. 1 760 3 25 13 01 | www.palmmountainresort.com | Budget–Moderate*

SAN DIEGO

PALM SPRINGS VISITORS CENTER
2901 N Palm Canyon Drive | tel. 1760 778 84 18 | www.visitpalmsprings.com

WHERE TO GO

JOSHUA TREE NATIONAL PARK ★ ●
(137 D–E 4–5) (*∭ G–H11*)

Cacti and coyotes dominate this desert park, created as early as 1936 where the Mojave and Colorado Deserts meet. In the uplands of the conservation area covering 1158 mi² near Hwy 62, entire for-

(136 C6) (*∭ F12*) **Meteorologists count over 300 sun days per year. San Diego cultivates its image as the epitome of the relaxed Californian lifestyle with its high quality of life thanks to many options for water sports and other types of exercise.**

The metropolis (pop. 3.3 million) is the birthplace of today's California. In 1769, taking advantage of a large natural port, the Spanish founded a fort here, as well as the *Mission San Diego de Alcalá*. The restored

The most spectacular rock formations in Joshua Tree National Park are the Giant Marbles

ests of Joshua trees, a type of yucca palm, grow up to 15 m/49.2 ft high here. Good hiking trails lead through Hidden Valley and Indian Cove. The best times to visit are: March/April for the desert bloom and late autumn. For a totally bizarre night in the desert, book one of the ten renovated retro-style trailers in INSIDER TIP *Hicksville (Joshua Tree | www.hicksville.com | Budget–Moderate).*

adobe houses from the Spanish era in the Old Town enjoy protected status as a State Park; and some of them may be visited.

Due to its extensive lagunes, the coast of San Diego County is 110 km/68 mi long. *Mission Bay, Mission Beach, Pacific Beach, Coronado* – the list of water-framed suburbs is long. Everywhere you'll find sandy beaches, surf spots, bike trails, terrace cafés and plenty of easy-going enjoyment of life. A particularly good example of the southern Californian lifestyle is the northern suburb of *La Jolla,* on a cliff above the Pacific.

SIGHTSEEING

BALBOA PARK
The park on a hill north of the city centre was founded as early as 1868 and in 1915/16 became the stage for the great Panama-Pacific Exposition, a world exhibition celebrating the opening of the Panama Canal. Today, the historic buildings house around a dozen museums, botanical gardens and the San Diego Zoo.

CABRILLO NATIONAL MONUMENT ↘↙
The headland far out west affords superb views across the bay and the city. Exhibitions at the *Visitor Center* illustrate the early history of California. *Daily 9am–5pm | admission $10 per car | Point Loma*

GASLAMP QUARTER
Pretty Victorian houses with art galleries and antique dealers, fashionable shops and popular bars. The historical district, originally called *New Town*, was laid out

in 1857 by Alonzo Horton, in an attempt to move the city closer to the sea. *Between Broadway and K Street*

MUSEUM OF CONTEMPORARY ART ↘↙
Minimalism, Pop Art, Californian art: in a new construction in La Jolla with sea views and also in the city centre, this museum shows off its splendid collection. *Thu–Tue 11am–5pm | admission $10 | 700 Prospect Street | La Jolla | www.mcasd.org*

SAN DIEGO ZOO ★ ◉
San Diego Zoo is one of the largest and best zoological gardens in the world, and its 4,000 animals include many rare species such as gorillas and other primates. The zoo is also well known for breeding successes with tigers and rare pandas. The habitats, adapted to the animals' needs, are exemplary: the zoo is attempting in (to date) a dozen biospheres to replicate the natural environment of the animals as closely as possible. As the grounds are extensive, the a cable car and bus (round trips) are helpful. *Daily 9am–6pm, longer in summer | admission $52 | Balboa Park | www.sandiegozoo.org*

SEA WORLD ★
A gigantic oceanarium covering some 148 acres and featuring polar bears, hundreds of penguins, sharks and a reconstructed coral reef. Hourly shows with orca whales, sea lions and jumping dolphins are controversial with animal rights activists. *In summer 9am–11pm, at other times 10am–5pm | admission $93, often cheaper internet offers | Pacific Beach | www.seaworld.com*

USS MIDWAY ●
Martial and gigantic: the 300 m/984 ft-long aircraft carrier with its widely pro-

truding landing deck is impressive, even at rest. Museum and guided tours. *Daily 10am–5pm | admission $20 | Navy Pier | 910 N Harbour Drive| www.midway.org*

FOOD & DRINK

BLIND BURRO

Chic terraced restaurant in the trendy district of East Village offering modern Mexican cuisine such as quinoa salad and lobster tacos. *639 J Street | tel. 1619 7 95 78 80 | Moderate*

CASA DE REYES

Smack bang in Old Town touristville, but serving very tasty Mexican specialities, fine margaritas and a shady terrace. *2754 Calhoun Street | tel. 1 619 2 20 50 40 | Budget–Moderate*

INSIDER TIP **CORVETTE**

Wonderful retro eatery with staff dolled up to the nines. *2965 Historic Decatur Road | tel. 619 5 42 14 76 | Budget–Moderate*

GEORGE'S AT THE COVE ⤜

Stylish fish restaurant boasting the finest views of the Pacific. Reservations essential! For a more laid-back vibe, choose the café and The Terrace. *1250 Prospect Street | La Jolla | tel. 1 858 4 54 42 44 | Expensive*

TOP OF THE MARKET ⤜

Enjoy fish dishes from all over the world with a view of the harbour. A more relaxed place is the *fish market* on the lower floor. *750 N Harbor Drive | tel. 1 619 2 32 34 74 | restaurant Expensive | fish market | Budget*

Deram city on the sea: San Diego, the third-largest metropolis in California

SAN DIEGO

A great choice of individual shops and sophisticated architecture: open-air shopping at Horton Plaza

SHOPPING

BAZAAR DEL MUNDO
Shops selling imports from Mexico and South America. *Old Town State Park | between Calhoun, Juan, Wallace and Mason Street*

CARLSBAD PREMIUM OUTLETS
Nearly 100 discount shops in a Mediterranean-style "village": Guess, Hilfiger, Gap, Puma, Ralph Lauren and many more. *Mon–Sat 10am–9pm, Sun 10am–7pm | 5620 Paseo Del Norte | Carlsbad*

HORTON PLAZA
The emblem of San Diego's city centre: a shopping centre colourfully thrown together borrowing from many architectural styles, with a lot of California flair. Some 150 shops are waiting for your business, plus depart-ment stores, cafés and cinemas. The many on-site restaurants are popular meeting places.

SPORTS & BEACHES

Silver Strand State Beach and *Coronado Beach (Coronado), Mission Beach, Tourmaline Surfing Park* and *La Jolla Cove (La Jolla)* as well as *Torrey Pines State Beach* in Del Mar are amongst the most beautiful beaches.

BIKING/INLINE SKATING
Hire from *Bike and Beyond (Coronado Ferry Landing | tel. 1 619 4 35 71 80)* and *Cheap Rentals (3689 Mission Blvd. | tel. 1 858 4 88 90 70)*.

WHALEWATCHING
In spring, the whales come up from their mating grounds off Baja California. For tours and harbour cruises: *Hornblower Cruises (San Diego | tel. 1 888 4 67 62 56)*,

WHERE TO STAY

HOTEL DEL CORONADO

In 1888, the "Del" was the first holiday hotel in southern California catering for wealthy guests. The house was the setting for the Monroe comedy "Some Like it Hot". The hotel boasts one of the most charming bars in all California – Babcock & Story, named after the two founders of the hotel. Daily guided tours on the history of the hotel with numerous anecdotes around the filming. *757 rooms | 1500 Orange Ave. | Coronado | tel. 1 619 4 35 66 11 | www.hoteldel.com | Expensive*

HUMPHREY'S HALF MOON INN ☽

Elegant resort featuring tropical gardens and its own marina, and a fine restaurant. *182 large suite rooms | 2303 Shelter Island Drive | tel. 1 619 2 24 34 11 | www.halfmooninn.com | Moderate–Expensive*

INSIDER TIP LA PENSIONE

Friendly small hotel on the northern side of the city centre in the Little Italy quarter. Clean rooms with kitchenette. *68 rooms | 606 W Date Street | tel. 1 619 2 36 80 00 | www.lapensionehotel.com | Budget*

INFORMATION

SAN DIEGO VISITORS BUREAU

996-B N Harbor Drive | tel. 1619 2 36 12 42 | www.sandiego.org

WHERE TO GO

BAJA CALIFORNIA (136 C6) (*ØØ F13*)

A detour to Mexico (20 km/12.4 mi south of San Diego, also accessible by tram) leads into the vibrant tourist mecca of *Tijuana* (pop. 1.7 million) and into lonely wild desert landscapes. Be aware that in recent years, drug wars and assaults have made Mexican border towns such as Tijuana dangerous for tourists. Hire cars are often subject to insurance restrictions.

SAN DIEGO SAFARI PARK

(136 C6) (*ØØ F12*)

Open-air enclosure with 450 endangered animal species in an artificial steppe landscape with swamps as well as a rainforest. *Daily 9am–7pm, shorter opening times in winter | admission $52 | 15500 San Pasqual Valley Road | Escondido | 45.06 km/28 mi from San Diego*

LOW BUDGET

Hotels in Palm Springs are up to 50 percent cheaper in summer because the heat deters many potential American visitors.

Mexican fare is still by far the cheapest in California. The best tacos come from the *Rubio's (www.rubios.com)* chain everywhere in southern California. Tip: fish tacos with salad and salsa – very tasty!

At first glance, the Go San Diego Card might not seem cheap, 1 day costing $89, 3 days $199, 7 days $279. However, in exchange you get harbour cruises, free entry to all museums in town, the San Diego Zoo as well as to the Midway aircraft carrier. www.smartdestinations.com

If you want to see all the big theme parks, save money with the *Citypass Southern California* coupon ticket, allowing you to visit the two Disney parks, Sea World and Legoland – slicing $ 100 off the regular admission price. www.citypass.com

DISCOVERY TOURS

1 CALIFORNIA AT A GLANCE

START: ① San Francisco
END: ① San Francisco

16 days
Driving time 50 hours
(without stops)

Distance:
🚗 3,000 km/1,864 mi

COSTS: fuel costs total approx. $240, rental bikes in Santa Barbara $36–$55 per day, rafting $75–$150, National Park Pass $80

WHAT TO PACK: hiking boots, swim gear, sun protection

IMPORTANT TIPS: The Tioga Pass is closed from late October to mid May, which means that you will have to take the detour over Lake Tahoe. Hwy. 1 is often closed for construction work.

Discover the many facets of California on this ideal route for first-time visitors. It covers the prettiest coastal stretches on the Pacific plus the deserts, mountains

Would you like to explore the places that are unique to this region? Then the Discovery Tours are just the thing for you – they include terrific tips for stops worth making, breathtaking places to visit, selected restaurants and fun activities. It's even easier with the Touring App: download the tour with map and route to your smartphone using the QR Code on pages 2/3 or from the website address in the footer below – and you'll never get lost again even when you're offline.

TOURING APP

→ p. 2/3

and vineyards to the west. The state's two most exciting cities, San Francisco and Los Angeles, are also on the agenda – and you won't miss out on a swim in one of California's cool *beachtowns*.

Plan on spending two days exploring ❶ **San Francisco** → p. 32: ride a cable car, stroll through Chinatown and along Fisherman's Wharf, tour Alcatraz and sail around the harbour. Then hit the road: **head south on US 101** to Silicon Valley → p. 43 and then **follow Highway 17** from San Jose towards the surfer and student town of Santa Cruz. Turn

DAY 1–2
❶ San Francisco

DAY 3
170 km/106 mi

Photo: Zabriskie Point, Death Valley

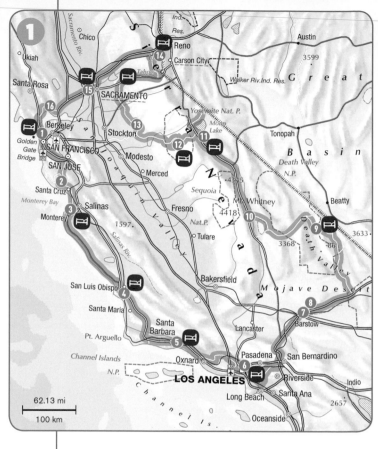

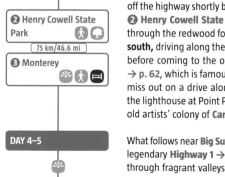

❷ Henry Cowell State Park

75 km/46.6 mi

❸ Monterey

off the highway shortly before you reach town to access the ❷ **Henry Cowell State Park**. Spend a half-hour walking through the redwood forest. Then take **Highway 1 further south,** driving along the dunes surrounding Monterey Bay before coming to the old harbour town of ❸ **Monterey** → **p. 62**, which is famous for its amazing aquarium. Don't miss out on a drive along the coast to Pacific Grove with the lighthouse at Point Pinos and walk on the beach in the old artists' colony of **Carmel → p. 62**.

DAY 4–5

What follows near **Big Sur** is the most beautiful stretch of the legendary **Highway 1 → p. 60**. Cruise along high cliffs and through fragrant valleys on this narrow and winding pan-

oramic route on the Pacific coast. Keep a lookout around **Cambria** for the elephant seals that often sun themselves on the beach. Today, the former mission town of ❹ **San Luis Obispo → p. 66** enchants visitors with its small, but fine vineyards in the Edna Valley – check out the **Baileyana Winery → p. 67**, for example, for a wine-tasting with a picnic. Broad beaches and high dunes await in the suburb of **Pismo Beach**. Some of the dunes are part of a nature conservation area, but in some places you can drive up to the beach. Afterwards, treat yourself to some freshly caught seafood at the rustic INSIDERTIP **Cracked Crab** *(751 Price Street | tel. 1 805 7 73 27 22 | Moderate).*

Continue along Highway 101: plan to spend a day in ❺ **Santa Barbara → p. 68** soaking up some sun and hitting the waves or biking to the Spanish mission that is the town's namesake. **At first, Highway 101 follows the coast,** but then it heads straight into the endless urban tapestry around ❻ **Los Angeles → p. 74.** You will need at least two days to properly explore the city: one for scouting VIPs in **Santa Monica → p. 80**, **Beverly Hills → p. 76** and **Hollywood → p. 78**, and one for delving into the fantasy worlds of **Universal Studios → p. 80** or **Disneyland → p. 88.**

Cross through **L.A. on the ten-lane highways I-10 and I-15 before heading east** into the desert. Give your credit card a good workout at some of the outlet malls in ❼ **Barstow** before the route becomes barren – and even hotter. Fans of the "Wild West" can pan for gold in the touristic ghost town of ❽ **Calico** *(daily 9am–5pm | admission $8)* on the I-15. If you want, you can switch to Tour 4 in **Baker** and take a detour to the glamorous Las Vegas → **p. 109** for a few days. Otherwise, the route continues directly **north from Baker via the highways 127 and 178** into the stony solitude of ❾ **Death Valley → p. 90.** Sunset or sunrise are the best times to enjoy the beauty of the salt lakes, dunes and multi-coloured eroded valleys. Careful: you should only attempt a hike in the morning when the temperatures are cooler.

Beyond the massive rift of Death Valley, **Highway 190 climbs across into Owens Valley**. Here, against the backdrop of the dramatically rising rock wall of the Sierra Nevada, **US 395 runs northwards**. Near Lone Pine, on the ❿ **Movie Road** northwest of town, you might recognise the bizarre sandstone formations because many early Western films were shot in the Alabama Hills. At ⓫ **Mono**

DAY 12

220 km/137 mi

⑫ Yosemite National Park

DAY 13–14

110 km/68 mi

⑬ Gold Country

275 km/171 mi

⑭ Lake Tahoe

DAY 15–16

200 km/124 mi

⑮ Sacramento

100 km/62 mi

⑯ Napa Valley

90 km/55.9 mi

❶ San Francisco

Lake → p. 73, **further north on US 395,** strange tuffstone pillars, a swim in the salty water at Navy Beach, the old silver mining town of **Bodie** → p. 73 and an overnight stay at the **Lee Vining** await. **Highway 120** will then take you into California's most famous conservation area, ⑫ **Yosemite National Park** → p. 71, whose spectacular glacier valleys and waterfalls can be explored on numerous hiking trails. During the winter months, you will have to circumvent Tioga Pass by driving via Lake Tahoe.

Highway 49 will then lead you north into ⑬ **Gold Country** → p. 58. Wild West towns such as **Jamestown** with its steam engine museum or the registered historic town of **Columbia** are perfect for some great snapshots. Plan on spending a day in **Placerville** on a refreshing whitewater rafting tour, e.g. with American Whitewater Expeditions → p. 115. **Highway 50 runs up to** ⑭ **Lake Tahoe** → p. 63, the largest mountain lake in North America. Alongside the hiking trails and idyllic natural landscapes, the area attracts visitors with its bright neon casinos situated on the Nevada border. **Head west on I-80** to the capital of California, ⑮ **Sacramento** → p. 64, with its very pretty old Wild West town centre on the river. Tip: the **Railroad Museum** offers trips on the nostalgic steam railway at the weekend. One last stop on this tour will surely delight your palate: **via I-80 and Highway 12**, you can drive into ⑯ **Napa Valley** → p. 52. Upscale Vineyards offering tastings lie along **Highway 29**. After buying a bottle or two, **follow SR 12, 121, 37 and US 101 back to** ❶ **San Francisco** – and arrive in proper style via the Golden Gate Bridge.

---

② A PARADISE FOR ADVENTURE SEEKERS: THE UNTAMED NORTH

START: ❶ San Francisco END: ❶ San Francisco	7 days Driving time (without stops) 30 hours
Distance: 🚗 1,800 km/1,119 mi	

COSTS: fuel costs, approx. $140
WHAT TO PACK: rain coat, hiking boots, jumper/fleece

IMPORTANT TIPS: The coast is often clouded in fog in July and August, so it is better to plan this tour for autumn or spring.

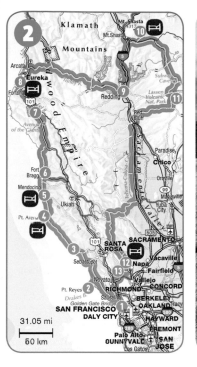

Fort Ross: Russian fur traders' settlement

Head off on a trip into the untamed and wild side of California in the north. Departing from San Francisco, this route follows the increasingly ragged Pacific coast northwards to gigantic redwood trees and upcountry to snow-capped volcanic cones. Then, on the way back to the south, you'll delve into the sweet world of Californian wine.

Only one route leaves **① San Francisco → p. 32 heading north and it takes you across the Golden Gate Bridge.** On the other side of the bay, **turn onto Highway 1**, which rolls past Bodega Bay with the windswept cliffs of **② Point Reyes → p. 54** and the **Sonoma Coast → p. 55**. This still untouched natural paradise is dotted with hiking trails and isolated beaches. From here, the route runs along the jagged Pacific coast due north. It's worth stopping to visit the reconstructed **③ Fort Ross** in the State Park of the same name; it was an outpost settled by Russian fur traders in 1812. Shortly thereafter, you will come to the treeless cape of **④ Point Arena** with its old INSIDER TIP **lighthouse** (7 rooms | tel. 1707

DAY 1

① San Francisco
> 100 km / 62 mi

② Point Reyes
> 120 km / 75 mi

③ Fort Ross
> 75 km / 46.6 mi

④ Point Arena

8 82 28 09 | www.pointarenalighthouse.com | *Moderate–Expensive*) and hiking trails to deserted beaches.

DAY 2–4

| 65 km/40.4 mi |
| **⑤ Mendocino** 🍴 🚍 |
| 140 km/87 mi |
| **⑥ Skunk Train** 🔔 |
| 100 km/62 mi |
| **⑦ Humboldt Redwoods State Park** 🌳 ❄ 🧍 |
| 100 km/62 mi |
| **⑧ Eureka** 🏢 🚍 |
| 230 km/143 mi |
| **⑨ Redding** 🏃 |
| 140 km/87 mi |
| **⑩ Mount Shasta** ❄ 🌳 ☕ 🚍 |

The next stop on Highway 1 is ⑤ **Mendocino** → p. 49, whose 19th-century timber houses provided the backdrop for the James Dean film East of Eden. Today, this artists' town is known for its fine restaurants. In neighbouring **Fort Bragg**, it's worth taking a trip with the steam-powered ⑥ **Skunk Train** → p. 49 **through the redwood forests to Willits**. Shortly thereafter, the impenetrability of the Lost Coast pushes Highway 1 back onto **Highway 101**, leading beyond Garberville to the **Avenue of the Giants** → p. 45, which makes for a gigantic natural spectacle in conjunction with the almost 100 yd. tall trees of the ⑦ **Humboldt Redwoods State Park** → p. 45. Just past Rio Dell, put in a stop to the small Victorian town of **Ferndale** → p. 46. After an overnight stay in ⑧ **Eureka** → p. 44, the most important town on the northern coast, follow **Highway 299**, which runs inland across the coastal mountains and the old gold-rush town of **Weaverville** to ⑨ **Redding** → p. 52. The stroll across the **Sundial Bridge** is quite an experience, even if you are not that into architecture. Travel quickly to the **north via the I-5,** passing the volcanic peak of ⑩ **Mount Shasta** → p. 50 at a height of 4,317 m/14,163 ft. Spend a lovely afternoon in one of the small cafés on Mount Shasta Blvd in the cosy town at the foot of the mountain.

DAY 5–7

| 215 km/134 mi |
| **⑪ Lassen Volcanic National Park** ❄ 🧍 🌳 |
| 400 km/249 mi |
| **⑫ Napa Valley** 🍷 🚍 |
| 33 km/20.5 mi |
| **⑬ Sonoma** ☕ 🛍 |
| 70 km/43.5 mi |
| **① San Francisco** |

Highway 89 winds from Mount Shasta into the thick forests of the Cascade Mountains on the way to the ⑪ **Lassen Volcanic National Park** → p. 48. Bizarre black basalt rocks surrounded by bubbling thermal and sulphurous springs serve as a reminder that our planet is still a bubbling cauldron beneath the surface. Thankfully, the hiking trails in the geothermal area of **Bumpass Hell** are well marked and quite safe. Take **Highway 36 and the I-5** back to the south, passing through Williams and Clearlake on **Highways 20, 53 and 29** on the way into the most famous wine-growing valley in the USA – ⑫ **Napa Valley** → p. 52, the heart of California's top-notch viniculture. **Highway 29** is the wine road, and it links **Calistoga**, a spa town with hot springs founded in 1859, and **Napa**. From here, take **Highway 12** to the pretty wine town of ⑬ **Sonoma** → p. 54. Sit in a café on the historic market square and pick up a bottle or two of wine as a souvenir. It is just about an hour's drive via **Highways 121, 37 and 101** back to ① **San Francisco**.

3 SURF'S UP, SUN'S OUT: THE HOT SOUTH AND ITS DESERTS

START: ❶ Los Angeles	6 days
END: ❶ Los Angeles	Driving time (without stops) 15 hours
Distance: 🚗 1,000 km/621 mi	

COSTS: fuel costs approx. $80, surfboard rental $40, cable car ride in Palm Springs $26

WHAT TO PACK: swim gear, sunscreen

IMPORTANT TIPS: When the temperatures rise in June, the coast of Southern California is often shrouded in fog.

This route runs along the surfing beaches of Southern California up to San Diego, a city that delights visitors with its relaxed holiday flair. It then crosses through the sun-dried Anza Borrego Desert of the Coachella Valley, which is home to the popular spa town of Palm Springs. After a hike in the Joshua Tree National Park, you will head back to L. A. This route is also perfect for a winter trip.

Once you have found your way out of the highway jungle of ❶ Los Angeles → p. 74, take the **I-5 south and then before you come to Santa Ana, turn onto the I-22 and the I-39 heading west** to California's surfers' paradise: ❷ **Huntington Beach** → p. 93. Right next door, up to 10,000 boats dock in the marina of elegant **Newport Beach**.

Highway 1, the Pacific Coast Highway, hugs the sandstone cliffs on the way to ❸ **Laguna Beach** → p. 92, which boasts an exciting mix of galleries, restaurants, boutiques

DAY 1

❶ Los Angeles

80 km/49.7 mi

❷ Huntington Beach

27 km/16.8 mi

❸ Laguna Beach

Upscale Laguna Beach attracts sun worshippers and art lovers

DAY 2–3

20 km/12.4 mi

④ San Juan Capistrano

50 km/31.1 mi

⑤ Carlsbad

65 km/40.4 mi

⑥ San Diego

DAY 4–5

140 km/87 mi

⑦ Anza Borrego Desert State Park

145 km/90 mi

and hotels. A fifteen minute **drive to the south will bring you to the harbour of Dana Point, where Del Obispo Street branches off inland to ④ San Juan Capistrano → p. 93**. Don't miss the mission itself that was founded in 1776. Take the **I-5 further south**, making a worthwhile stop in **⑤ Carlsbad** (Legoland for families, the outlet mall for shoppers) before continuing along the coast. Elegant villas and long beaches line **Highway 1** down to **La Jolla**, the chic beach suburb of **⑥ San Diego → p. 95** situated atop a cliff. Alongside the city centre with its stylish Horton Plaza shopping centre, the Gaslamp Quarter and Balboa Park, the city is home to one of the world's most beautiful zoos.

Leave San Diego on the **I-8, then cross over to Highway 79 North and then to Highway 78 East** to drive through **⑦ Anza Borrego Desert State Park**. The park's barren cactus landscapes and good hiking paths blossom in the spring in the truest sense of the word thanks to countless wildflowers. **Head to Borrego Springs and continue north on Highway 86** through date plantations and along **Salton Sea**, a hostile saline, and access, and the **Coachella Valley via Highway 111**. In this sunny desert valley full of large date palm plantations, more than 90 golf courses crowd into an area of less than 19 mi². Make sure to check out **8 The Living Desert → p. 94**, a nature park and zoo that expertly shows what lives in the desert. In **9 Palm Springs → p. 93**, you also shouldn't miss out on the view from the peak of **Mount San Jacinto**; the cable car with rotating cars climbs the mountain in just 20 minutes. A stroll through the nice shops on **Palm Canyon Drive** (Thursdays **INSIDER TIP** *Villagefest* street fair with live music) provides a contrast to the natural highlights of the region.

Hop on the I-10 and drive east to Cottonwood Springs Road, which will take you north into the desert and to the southern entrance of the **10 Joshua Tree National Park → p. 95**. Pass by **Ocotillo Patch** and the **Cholla Cactus Garden** and take **Pinto Basin Road and Park Boulevard** into the western part of the park that sits at a higher elevation where yuccas grow over 12 m/39.4 ft tall. From **Keys View**, you can enjoy the sweeping view over Coachella Valley as far as the San Jacinto Mountains. **Quail Springs Road** will lead you back out of the 927 mi² park near the little town of Joshua Tree. For the fastest route back to civilization, take **Highway 62 and the I-10** to one of the largest outlet malls in California, the **11 Cabazon Outlets**. Depending on the time of day and traffic, it will take you 1.5 to 2 hours on the **I-10 to get back to 1 Los Angeles**.

8 The Living Desert

20 km/12.4 mi

9 Palm Springs

DAY 6

140 km/87 mi

10 Joshua Tree National Park

150 km/93 mi

11 Cabazon Outlets

150 km/93 mi

1 Los Angeles

4 INTO THE DESERT: LAS VEGAS AND DEATH VALLEY

START: **1 Los Angeles**	6 days
END: **1 Los Angeles**	Driving time
Distance:	(without stops)
🚗 1,400 km/870 mi	22 hours

COSTS: fuel costs $110, show in Las Vegas $80–$150
WHAT TO PACK: sunscreen, hiking boots, cooler and drinks

IMPORTANT TIPS: The summer heat in Death Valley is extreme. It is better to plan this route for autumn, winter or spring. The hotels in Las Vegas are much cheaper from Sundays to Thursdays than at the weekend.

This tour is a true Californian desert experience in the hot, aptly named Death Valley with a detour into the neon-lit metropolis of Las Vegas. It can easily be added on as an extension to one of the other tours.

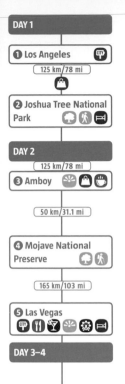

DAY 1	
❶ Los Angeles 🏙️	
125 km/78 mi 🛍️	
❷ Joshua Tree National Park 🌳🚶‍♂️🚌	
DAY 2	
125 km/78 mi	
❸ Amboy 🌞🏨🏠☕	
50 km/31.1 mi	
❹ Mojave National Preserve 🌳🚶‍♂️	
165 km/103 mi	
❺ Las Vegas 🏙️🍽️🎿🌞🎰🚌	
DAY 3–4	

Leaving from ❶ **Los Angeles → p. 74**, the **I-10** will take you into the desert in almost no time at all -- unless you give into the temptation of the countless shops at the outlet mall **Cabazon** . Shortly thereafter, exit onto **SR 62 heading north** onto the plateau of the ❷ **Joshua Tree National Park → p. 95**, where you should plan to spend the night (this is a good place to connect with Tour 3). A hike through the park, e.g. in Hidden Valley, is particularly beautiful in April when the cacti bloom. From here, things will start to get lonely: on the eastern edge of the desert town of **Twentynine Palms**, drive along **Amboy Road** across barren mountains and a usually dry salt lake to ❸ **Amboy**. This one-horse town is one of the last authentic stops on the legendary **Route 66**. You simply must take a souvenir photo in front of the sign for **Roy's Cafe**; matching t-shirts and chilled Coke cans are sold inside. **In Amboy, go right, due east, and then left on the next street, Kelbaker Road,** into the ❹ **Mojave National Preserve → p. 91** and the little town of **Kelso**. The old railway station has been turned into the Visitors' Center for the national park. Take **Morning Star Mine Road east to the I-15,** which will bring you across the border with the neighbouring state of Nevada and to ❺ **Las Vegas**.

The famous gambling town merits at least two days (and more importantly three nights) – for great shows and evenings at the blackjack table or meals at innovative restaurants before relaxing at the pool of an (often surprisingly inexpensive) casino hotel on **Las Vegas Boulevard**, the famous "Strip". At the **Venetian**, gondolas glide along the water just like in Venice, and at the **Paris** you can head to

Welcome to fabulous Las Vegas!

the top of the replica Eiffel Tower. Fantastic fountains dance to music in front of the **Bellagio** while gigantic crystal chandeliers grace the lobby of the ultra-chic **Cosmopolitan**. Bask in the noble Roman flair of **Caesars Palace** or take in the Egyptian ambiance of the **Luxor** with its huge pyramids and even a sphinx replica. Don't forget to check out the old **Downtown**, where free light shows take place every night on a giant dome of light above **Fremont Street**.

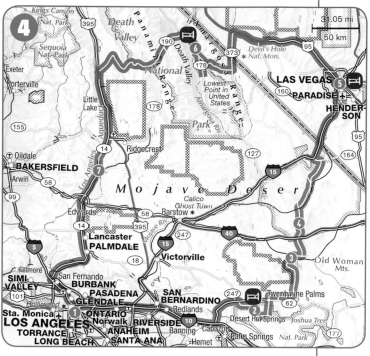

After gambling the night away, leave Las Vegas on **Highway 95 North**, passing by the former nuclear testing zones of the US military, to the seemingly deserted town of **Amargosa Valley**. From here, take **Highways 373, 127 and 190** into ❻ **Death Valley → p. 90**. It is an absolute must to drive from **Furnace Creek** in the heart of the valley to **Badwater** – a bizarre, usually dried-up salt lake at the INSIDER TIP lowest point in the western hemisphere. After passing by the massive sand dunes of **Stovepipe Wells**, the route continues on **Highway 190** up the western flank of the valley and on into **Owens Valley** at the edge of the Sierra Nevada Mountains. **US 395** runs south from here, surrounded by the dramatic backdrop of snow-capped peaks, to **Highway 14, which branches off to the town of Mojave**. Say goodbye to the desert with a short hike at ❼ **Red Rock Canyon** on the Hagen Trail or the Red Cliffs Trail. From Mojave, take **Highway 14 and the I-5** and you will be back in ❶ **Los Angeles** in half a day.

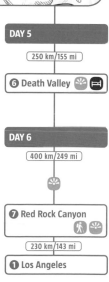

DAY 5

250 km/155 mi

❻ Death Valley

DAY 6

400 km/249 mi

❼ Red Rock Canyon

230 km/143 mi

❶ Los Angeles

SPORTS & ACTIVITIES

Beaches, mountains and lakes, raging rivers, sunburnt deserts, and pleasant temperatures all year round: California has it all. Add to this a population that venerates fitness and health to a near-religious extent and is open to everything that's new.

Both components taken together have turned the Golden State into a leisure paradise and laboratory for ever-new trend sports – with one great goal and one only: fun and action. The rivers for instance are not just there to be admired, but are a playground for kayakers and white-water rafters. Take off from mountains or dunes by hang glider, and explore fascinating underwater worlds just off the coast. Visitors who desire only an occasional bout of sports activity will be as happy as fans of extreme sports. In California the motto is always: sweat may flow, but doesn't have to, the main thing is to have fun!

CYCLING

California offers every kind of terrain, from blazing hot desert to oxygen-starved mountain passes, from curvy coastlines to bike tours right through the heart of San Francisco. Bike hire can be found everywhere in towns and cities, as well as resorts *(prices $25–60 per day)*.

In San Francisco in particular, mountain bikers have come to the right place: it was on Mount Tamalpais in Marin County that their chunky-tyred means of transport was invented, and to this day, the

Photo: Mountain biking in Death Valley

California sets the top trends in sports, and fitness is a religion: ideal conditions for an activity holiday

800 m/2,625 ft "Mount Tam" is a mecca of the biking scene. Mount Tamalpais and the Muir Woods make ideal day trips from San Francisco. Hire your bike (or your e-bike) at *Blazing Saddles* (*2715 Hyde Street | tel. 1 415 20 88 88 | www.blazingsaddles.com*). Other haunts of the *fat-tire* community are *Mammoth Lakes* with the famous *Kamikaze Trail* and the passes of the *High Sierra*. Bike hire: *Footloose Sports* (*3043 Main Street | Mammoth Lakes | tel. 1 760 9 34 24 00 | www.footloosesports.com*).

GOLF

Around the golfing bastion of *Palm Springs* alone there are over 80 courses, the whole state has hundreds. To tee off on legendary courses such as *Pebble Beach* right on the Pacific at Monterey expect to pay a whopping $500 in green fees, while on the many less well-known (but no less beautiful) courses, fees hover around the reasonable $50 to $150 range. Your hotel concierge can usually arrange even short-notice *tee-*

times. For more information see *www. golfcalifornia.com* and *www.centralcoast golftrail.com.*

HIKING & TREKKING

California's wild nature offers trails for both day walkers and extreme hikers. In the national and state parks in particular the trails are exceptionally well maintained (pick up exact maps from the visitor centres). The most famous long-distance trail is the  *Pacific*

HORSERIDING

In the north of California in particular, signs by the roadside often point to opportunities for *trail riding* – also for beginners. Day rides and longer treks into the wild country of the *John Muir* and *Ansel Adams Wilderness* of the High Sierra are on offer at the *High Sierra Pack Station (www.highsierrapackstations.com),* shorter hacks into the High Sierra through *Mammoth Lakes Pack Outfit (Mammoth Lakes | tel. 1 888 4 75 87 47 | www.mam*

Racing down the falls: whitewater rafting on the Tuolumne River

Crest Trail, which follows the ridge of the mountains from Mexico to Canada. Sections such as the high-alpine  *John Muir Trail* in Yosemite National Park are also pretty. Other trails with far-reaching views: the half-day  *Lassen Peak Trail* or the trails on  *Mount Shasta.* Information: *Pacific Crest Trail Association (1331 Garden Highway | Sacramento | tel. 1 916 2 85 18 46 | www.pcta.org).*

mothpack.com). **INSIDER TIP** Scenic hacks in a quiet beach park on the Pacific, the *Salinas River State Park* just north of Monterey, are organised through *Monterey Bay Equestrian (Salinas | tel. 1 831 6 63 57 12 | www.montereybayequestrian.com).*

PARAGLIDING

There's nothing more beautiful than to

float in the balmy Californian air – no problem, even for beginners. Several good schools offer courses in paragliding and hang gliding. And you don't even need any training to enjoy a INSIDER TIP tandem flight across the Santa Barbara Mountains. Book at *Fly Above All (2707 De La Vina Street | Santa Barbara | tel. 1 805 9 65 37 33 | www.fly aboveall.com)*. Flights near San Francisco are organised by *Bay Area Hang Gliding (information hotline 1 408 65 66 79 | bayareahanggliding.com)*.

RAFTING

If you've ever taken part in a rafting expedition through rapids many feet high, you'll know all about ice-cold water between skin and clothing, huge doses of adrenaline and the great team spirit involved. In California over 50 rivers offer wild rides through foaming H2O. Particularly popular with rafters are the rivers on the western flanks of the Sierra Nevada, such as the *American River* or the *Tuolumne River*.

The *Upper Klamath River* on Mount Shasta should only be attempted by experienced white-water fans. *American Whitewater Expeditions (Sunland | tel. 1 800 8 25 32 05 | www.americanwhitewater. com)* organises half-day to two-day trips on the American River. Rafting on the *American, Stanislaus* and *Kaweah Rivers* is arranged through *Beyond Limits Adventures (Riverbank | tel. 1 530 6 22 05 53 | www.rivertrip.com)*.

SKIING & SNOWBOARDING

With an average of 18 m/59.1 ft of snowfall each winter, the Sierra Nevada can probably satisfy any winter sports enthusiast – especially as the sun often shines for a long time after some snowstorms at the beginning of winter. The most popular skiing areas are *Squaw Valley* and *Heavenly Valley* on Lake Tahoe, as well as *Mammoth Mountain* on the eastern side of the mountains. Detailed information: *tel. 1 415 3 89 10 00 | skicalifornia.org* and *skilaketahoe.com*

SURFING

Surfing is the Californian sport par excellence: elegantly sliding down high walls of water on a slim board. Californian boys and girls surf wherever the waves break evenly and in a long ripple. The most famous surfing beaches in California are in the south: *Bolsa Chica State Park, Topanga State Beach,* ● *Huntington Beach, Las Tunas State Beach and Surfrider Beach, Hermosa Beach* and *Manhattan State Beach*. You can take classes and hire boards for $25–50 per day nearly everywhere. For information see *www. surfline.com*.

WELLNESS

● While the Californians didn't invent yoga and massages, they have taken a leading role in the feelgood & relax trend of the past few years. These days, every resort hotel has a spa too, which offers massages with hot stones, bodywraps with seaweed or desert herbs, or relaxation with fragrant ayurvedic oils and gentle yoga exercises. Hotel spas are also often embedded into the landscape in eye-catching designs, e.g. the Fairmont Sonoma Mission Inn & Spa (see p. 54) with its own mineral springs, the Spa Solage (*www.solageca listoga.com*) in the adjacent Napa Valley with volcanic mud treatments or the ultra luxurious Cal a vie Spa (*www.cal-a-vie.com*) in southern California. Information: *www.spafinder.com*

TRAVEL WITH KIDS

Americans love children. The family is sacred here, which is why kids are taken everywhere. And the state's infrastructure is perfectly adapted to their needs.

Apart from the casinos in the glittering city of Las Vegas, all places of tourist interest are geared up for children. Restaurants will wave their *menu for kids* and the hotels their *"kids stay for free"* offers. Swimming pools, children's programmes in national parks and playgrounds in shopping malls make a family trip a pleasure.

You should definitely schedule more time when you travel around with kids, though, as you'll invariably come across adventure pools, imaginatively laid-out mini-golf courses and reconstruc-

ted Wild West towns. Last but not least they help take the sting out of what are sometimes long distances. If you have a bit of time on your trip, schedule an average of no more than 150 km/93 mi or so per day.

Then there are of course all the famous entertainment parks, which leave kids open-mouthed in admiration – and often not just the kids. There's *Disneyland*, there's *Sea World*, the rollercoasters of *Knott's Berry Farm* or *Six Flags Magic Mountain* and the *Universal Film Studios*. California's beaches are playgrounds for any age, and the national parks, too, promise unforgettable memories for everyone, of chipmunks around the picnic areas and camping below the stars.

Photo: Bathing fun at Laguna Beach

California dreamin' for the little ones: they'll never forget their experiences in the Golden State

SAN FRANCISCO

CABLE CAR MUSEUM ● (U E2) *(M e2)*
Alongside a noisy juddering trip aboard the Cable Car the kids will also enjoy the Cable Car Museum. Here at the operational headquarters of the historic rack-and-pinion railway, the more than 140-year-old technology is explained in a graphic and entertaining way, and you can see the massive cable reels that power the cable cars in action. *April–Oct daily 10am–6pm, at other times daily 10am–5pm | free admission | 1201 Mason Street/ Washington Street | www.cablecarmuse um.org*

CHILDREN'S CREATIVITY MUSEUM
(U F2) *(M f2)*
Silicon Valley for kids: record music, film videos, and design computer games at the high tech studios here that have been adapted for kids – a great experience for ages 5 and up. *Wed–Sun 10am–4pm | admission $12 | 221 Fourth Street | www. creativity.org*

THE NORTH

SIX FLAGS DISCOVERY KINGDOM
(134 A1) (🛱 B7)

A successful mix of fun park and oceanarium, with spectacular roller coasters, sea lion shows, walrus experience and shark watching. 50 km/31.1 mi north of San Francisco. *In summer daily from 10.30am | admission $68, children $43 | Freeway I-80/SR-37 | Vallejo | www.sixflags.com/discoverykingdom*

CENTRAL CALIFORNIA

LAKE TAHOE (133 E4–5) (🛱 D6)

California's prettiest mountain lake is an ideal activity playground for families with children, from paddling in a canoe via waterskiing to parasailing. Always a hit with the kids: trips on the paddleboat steamer *Tahoe Queen*. You'll find the largest selection of sports equipment for hire at *Zephyr Cove Marina (tel. 1 800 2 38 24 63 | www.zephyrcove.com)*. Never steered a rubber raft through rapids before? Make a start on the *Truckee River*. The Truckee, vibrant rather than temperamental, is a rafting zone suitable for the entire family. *Truckee River Raft Rental (185 River Road | Tahoe City | tel. 1 530 5 83 01 23 | www.truckeeriverraft.com)*.

MONTEREY BAY AQUARIUM
(134 A3) (🛱 B8)

With over 350,000 marine dwellers, a three-storey water tank and a fantastic exhibition on deep-sea fish, this is a truly stunning underwater world. The most eye-catching VIPs here are the sharks, barracudas, giant marine turtles and sea otters. *In summer daily 9.30am–6pm, at other times 10am–7pm | admission $50, children $30 | 886 Cannery Row | Monterey | www.montereybayaquarium.org*

PAN FOR GOLD

Great fun for kids: buy a washing pan at the gift shop of Nevada City (133 D4) (🛱 C6) or Sonora (133 E6) (🛱 D7), and head for the nearest river! You never know, after some thorough shaking, the glittering object on the bottom of the pan might well be a nugget. If you don't

Encounter at the shark pool at Monterey Bay Aquarium, one of the largest in the world

trust your own instinct entrust yourself to one of the professional companies. They'll tell you how it's done and will throw in a good number of great stories. *Gold Prospecting Adventures (costs depending on length of tour $30–150 | Jamestown | tel. 1 209 9 84 46 53 | www.goldprospecting.com).*

SANTA CRUZ BEACH BOARDWALK
(134 A2) (*Ω B8*)

A wonderfully old-fashioned fun park right on the beach: wooden rollercoasters from 1911, merry-go-rounds, shopping arcades. The nearby Neptune's Kingdom is a theme park with a huge mini-golf course. In summer *Mon–Fri from 10am, Sat/Sun from 9am | free admission, fun rides $4–7 | Hwy. 1 | Santa Cruz | www.beachboardwalk.com*

WHALE WATCHING (135 D6) (*Ω D11*)

The north-south migration of the grey whales takes place between December and May. The best places for observing them from dry land are *Point Reyes National Seashore, Mendocino Headlands State Park, Carmel* and *Santa Barbara*. The season for humpback and blue whales runs from June to November. Boat trips allow you to experience the gentle giants close up. Some of these boats leave from Santa Barbara: *Condor Cruises, Sea Landing (in spring from $50, children $30, otherwise $99, children $50 | 301 W Cabrillo Blvd. | Santa Barbara | tel. 1 805 8 82 00 88).*

LOS ANGELES

PAGE MUSEUM/LA BREA TAR PITS
(138 C3) (*Ω E11*)

Sabre-toothed tigers, prehistoric lions and mammoths once drowned in the tar swamp of La Brea – and have risen again today in life size. The open-air enclosure features the reconstructions, the museum the skeletons. *Daily 9.30am–5pm | admission $12, children $5 | 5801 Wilshire Blvd. | www.tarpits.org*

SIX FLAGS MAGIC MOUNTAIN
(136 A–B4) (*Ω E11*)

Somewhat out of the way, but well worth a visit for roller-coaster and high-tech fans: the latest acquisition, Battle for Metropolis, is the hottest babe in interactive 3-D technology. Other *rollercoasters*, with names like *Scream, Colossus* or *Ninja* will also have your hair standing on end. Next door, *Hurricane Harbor* is a tropical water park with 10 super slides. *In summer daily from 10.30am | admission Magic Mountain $80, children $55, Hurricane Harbor $43, children $35 | Valencia | Freeway I-5, exit Magic Mountain Parkway | www.sixflags.com*

THE SOUTH

LEGOLAND CALIFORNIA
(136 C5–6) (*Ω F12*)

The adventure park built around the famous little plastic bricks, now in California too: visit the USA in miniature or go on safari through a Lego jungle. Super fun – especially for younger children. In summer daily usually 10am–8pm, at other times *Thu–Mon 10am–5pm | admission $95, children $89 | Carlsbad | Freeway I-5, Cannon Road Exit | www.legoland.com*

INSIDER TIP THE NEW CHILDREN'S MUSEUM (136 C6) (*Ω F12*)

How do animals see the world, and how do you create ghost masks? A museum combining perception, art and children. *Mon, Wed–Sat 10am–4pm, Sun noon–4pm | admission both adults and children $13 | 200 W Island Ave. | San Diego | www.thinkplaycreate.org*

FESTIVALS & EVENTS

"Half of all mad people live within a 50 miles radius of Los Angeles", US president Harry Truman once sighed. The Californians have long taken this as a compliment – a fact reflected in their many and often crazy festivals.

EVENTS

JANUARY

With its flower-bedecked floats, the *Tournament of Roses Parade* in Pasadena is California's prettiest New Year's party; as a follow-up watch the college football match broadcast country-wide.

FEBRUARY

The Chinatowns of San Francisco and L.A. celebrate the *Chinese New Year* with paper dragons and parades.

MARCH

Snowfest in Tahoe City: the biggest winter carnival in California offers snow sculptures, parades and a dip in icy-cold Lake Tahoe. *www.tahoesnowfestival.com*

The *LA Marathon* in Los Angeles, followed by over 100 live music groups along the way, is the first big marathon of the year. *www.lamarathon.com*

APRIL

Coachella Valley Music and Arts Festival: California's largest music festival, in the desert. *www.coachella.com*

On ✪ *Earth Day,* 22 April, all kinds of eco actions in many cities. www.earthday.org

For 100 years, cowboys have been riding wild bulls and broncos at *Clovis Rodeo* in Central Valley. *www.clovisrodeo.com*

MAY

On 5 May, *Cinco de Mayo*, the Mexican immigrants celebrate their cultural heritage – particularly colourful in L.A.

Sacramento Music Festival: Downtown and Old Sacramento turn into an open-air stage for jazz, blues and zydeco.

✪ *Grand Kinetic Championship:* crazy 3-day race with home-made and human-powered vehicles on the northern Californian coast. *www.kineticgrandchampionship.com*

JUNE

Cotton Candy and *Country Music:* end of the month, at the INSIDER TIP ▶ *San Diego County Fair* experience a traditional American fair

At the end of June, gays and lesbians in San Francisco and West Hollywood celebrate ★ ● *Pride Day* with parades.

There are hundreds of festivals for Californians to celebrate their state – and themselves, why not?

JULY

Independence Day (4 July) is celebrated with parades, fireworks and music.

At the end of July, the world's best surfers compete at the **US Open of Surfing** in Huntington Beach in front of 500,000 fans. *www.vansusopenofsurfing.com*

AUGUST

The founders of Santa Barbara are honoured with parades and culinary treats at the INSIDER TIP ***Old Spanish Days Fiesta***. *www.oldspanishdays-fiesta.org*
County Fair, a nostalgic funfair, in Ferndale. *www.humboldtcountyfair.org*

SEPTEMBER

Sausalito Art Festival: artists from all over the world. *www.sausalitoartfestival.org*
The top set of the international jazz scene plays at the ***Monterey Jazz Festival***.

OCTOBER

Oldtimer fans drive in San Bernardino to the ***Route 66 Rendezvous*** in their highly polished vehicles. *rendezvoustoroute66.com*

On ***Halloween***, children in shrill costumes swarm around the neighbourhood.

DECEMBER

Colourful lights in marinas like Newport Beach for the *Christmas Boat Parades*.

PUBLIC HOLIDAYS

1 Jan	New Year's Day
3rd Mon in Jan	Martin Luther King Jr. Day
3rd Mon in Feb	President's Day
31 March	Cesar Chavez Day
4th Mon in May	Memorial Day
4 July	Independence Day
1st Mon in Sept	Labor Day
11 Nov	Veteran's Day
4th Thu/Fri	Thanksgiving Day in Nov & Day after
25 Dec	Christmas Day

LINKS, BLOGS, APPS & MORE

LINKS & BLOGS

www.santamonica.com, www.santabarbara.com Many Californian tourist boards have excellent websites – of which these are only two examples – with videos, blogs and apps to download. A look at the site of the relevant Visitor's Bureau is essential when planning to stay somewhere for a few days

www.swellinfo.com The perfect site for watersports fans: up-to-date surf reports, blogs, podcasts and videos, mainly about the northern Californian surfing community. Also contacts for surfshops and links to the surf scene's social media

www.seeing-stars.com Where do the stars eat, where do they live, when was that movie made and where? Answers to pretty much all your Hollywood-related questions

www.yelp.com The triumphal march of the 'Yelpers' began in San Francisco: completely normal people who compiled witty and sometimes malicious reviews of shoops, coffee shops and restaurants

www.sfgate.com The extensive website of San Fran's biggest daily newspaper maintains several blogs and social media channels on the arts and up-to-date topics relating to the city. Plus good restaurant reviews and a search function

www.twitter.com/michaelbauer1 San Francisco's most famous restaurant critic reviews restaurant novelties and classics

www.laweekly.com The latest from Los Angeles and San Francisco: city scene, stars, vernissages, fashion trends, music and politics – numerous blogs

californiathroughmylens.com Blog by California resident Josh telling you all about his state – from national parks to adventures, roads, restaurants and cities. Includes a section on "bizarre" sights like haunted or abandoned houses

Regardless of whether you are still researching your trip or already in California: these addresses will provide you with more information, videos and networks to make your holiday even more enjoyable

VIDEOS & MUSIC

travelbydrone.com The video collection is generally well-known, but what is particularly fascinating are the numerous magnificent drone flights along the West coast and in the Nationalparks

short.travel/kal1 A crazy race through the streets of San Francisco, guaranteed to give you sweaty palms

hbcams.com Several live webcams with views of Huntington Beach Pier – and, depending on the swell, of the surfers

californiathroughmylens.com Blog by California resident Josh telling you all about his state – from national parks to adventures, roads, restaurants and cities. Includes a section on "bizarre" sights like haunted or abandoned houses

short.travel/kal2 Cool little promotional videos about the lifestyle on the Pacific coast

APPS

www.livenation.com Central ticket sales for concert tours of the big stars and hundreds of clubs and stages in California. With iPhone app and facebook service: www.facebook.com/livenation

Pocket Ranger iPhone app for download with detailed descriptions of the Californian State Parks and their hiking trails

opentable Very useful and comprehensive site for restaurant reservations, in San Francisco and Los Angeles in particular, also at very short notice. Plus apps for iPhone, Android and Blackberry

Golden Gate Park iPhone app Paths, animals, attractions – the versatile iPhone App by the Academy of Sciences shows everything about the Park, even in 3-D

www.mousewait.com Fun app showing waiting times for attractions in Disneyland. Works well as a conversation starter while you wait in line

TRAVEL TIPS

ARRIVAL

✈ The non-stop flight from London takes around 10.5 hours. In the low season tickets start at £400, in high season (in summer) at £740. One of the best-value airlines is *Continental Airlines (www.continental.com)*, flying non-stop from London to Los Angeles. *Virgin Atlantic* also offers cheap non-stop flights. Many US airports offer direct flights from $80 to Los Angeles or San Francisco.

LOS ANGELES

Flights from Europe and the US east coast land at *Los Angeles International Airport (LAX)*. The shuttle buses of the hire-car companies leave in front of the baggage retrieval and take you to the pick-up stations outside the airport area. The best bus connection into the city centre is the *Super Shuttle (www.supershuttle. com)*, which runs small buses as a collective taxi to any address in town. Pick-up is at the traffic island in front of the building. Hotels near the airport usually have their own shuttle buses. Due to the long distances, a taxi can be expensive, so it's best to arrange a flat fee. To give you an idea: a taxi to Hollywood costs at least $40.

SAN FRANCISCO

Flights from Europe and the US east coast land at *San Francisco International Airport (SFO)*. Due to the airport's proximity to the city centre and the lack of reasonably priced parking facilities it's a good idea to wait with hiring a car until you want to do a day trip or travel on. Several small buses/shared taxis, such as the *Super Shuttle (www.supershut tle.com)* leave from the traffic islands in front of the terminals and will take you for around $17–25 to any destination in the city area. A taxi to downtown costs around $40, the fast subway connection by *Bart (www.bart.gov)* only $10; however, this option shares the same drawback as the *SamTrans* city buses of being a bit cumbersome for transporting luggage.

RESPONSIBLE TRAVEL

It doesn't take a lot to be environmentally friendly whilst travelling. Don't just think about your carbon footprint whilst flying to and from your holiday destination but also about how you can protect nature and culture abroad. As a tourist it is especially important to respect nature, look out for local products, cycle instead of driving, save water and much more. If you would like to find out more about eco-tourism please visit: *www.ecotourism.org*

BARRIER-FREE TRAVEL

Thanks to numerous statutory regulations, California is very well-equipped to welcome disabled travellers: all holiday hotels and motels have rooms accessible for the disabled; there are lifts everywhere, ramps for wheelchair users, special handicapped parking and also disabled toilets in all public buildings. Car rental firms such as Alamo, Avis and Hertz will provide rental cars with manual operation.

From arrival to weather

Your holiday from start to finish: the most important addresses and information for your California trip

CAMPING & HOSTELS

The most beautiful campsites are located in the state parks. Reservations are possible from seven months ahead *(fee: $8)* through *Reserve America (tel. 1 800 4 44 72 75 | www.reservecalifornia.com)*. For details of the individual parks, see the website of the *Department of Parks and Recreation: www.parks.ca.gov*.

AYH Youth Hostels should be reserved in advance. The hostels are often situated at particularly picturesque places. Also recommended for families. A list is available from bookshops or at *www.hiusa.org*.

CAR HIRE

SALOON CARS

Experience tells us that rental cars are cheapest when booked from home, which also usually allows you to choose a different drop-off location without extra cost. Very reasonable tariffs for round trips of one or several weeks are available from broker companies such as *Holiday Autos*. It's well worth comparing prices. The rental car companies have branches at all major airports.

CAMPERVANS

Reserve your vehicle early, i.e. ideally from home. However, you might be lucky at short notice too and get a campervan. *El Monte RV Rentals* with branches outside Los Angeles and San Francisco offers *RVs (recreation vehicles)* starting at $700 per week. Shoulder season prices can be up to 40 per cent lower. Book through travel agents or *www.elmonterv.com*.

CURRENCY CONVERTER

£	USD	USD	£
1	1.27	1	0.78
2	2.54	2	1.56
3	3.81	3	2.34
5	6.35	5	3.90
7	8.89	7	5.46
10	12.70	10	7.80
25	31.75	25	19.50
75	95.25	75	58.50
100	127	100	78

For current exchange rates see www.xe.com

CLIMATE

Summers in California are dry. The winter brings longed-for rain and at higher attitudes snow. In San Francisco, due to the frequent fog, the summer months are cooler than the more pleasant months of May/June and September. The warmest month is September, when the mercury rises to over 20 °C/68°F. In winter, the milder south of California registers top temperatures between 10°C/50°F and 18°C/64 °F, between July and September 23°C/73°F and over. In the desert, extreme values reach over 50°C/122°F.

CONSULATES & EMBASSIES

UK CONSULATE

– 2029 Century Park East | Suite 1350 | Los Angeles, CA 90067 | tel. 1 310 789 00 31 | www.ukinusa.fco.gov.uk
– 1 Sansome Street / Suite 850 / San Francisco, CA 94104 / tel. 1 415 617 13 00 / www.ukinusa.fco.gov.uk/sf

CUSTOMS

Exempt from customs duty on arrival are personal equipment, 200 cigarettes, 1 litre of spirits and presents with a value of up to $100. The import of foodstuffs is limited (no sausage, fresh fruit or fresh plant products, not even as travel provisions). For duty-free import back into the EU, you're allowed (per person): 1 litre of spirits or 2 litres of wine, 200 cigarettes, 50 grammes of perfume and other goods up to a total value of £350.

DRIVING

In the US, roads are divided into *County Routes, State* and *US Highways* up to *Interstate* highways, of which some are toll roads. The top speeds are between 88 km/h/55 mph and 112 km/h/70 mph. Traffic rules and signs in den US are roughly equivalent to those in the British Isles.

Some particularities: at crossroads you may turn right at red lights; the *3-way* or *4-way stop,* a crossroads with stop signs for traffic coming from all sides, organises priority according to the principle of who arrives first, goes first (following the sequence of arrival at the stopping line); overtaking on the right is permitted on multi-lane roads; when school buses stop at the side of the road with their red hazard lights on, traffic from either direction has to stop.

If you have a breakdown, contact your car rental company. Maps and information are available from the *AAA (American Automobile Association), service number 800 2 22 43 57.*

FOR BOOKWORMS AND FILM BUFFS

American Graffiti – 1973 cult movie about the rock'n' roll generation of the sixties; filmed in Modesto, the hometown of director George Lucas

Tales of the City – In this humorous, iconic book series of orignially six volumes (but by now there are several sequels), Armistead Maupin tells of life in San Francisco

Surferboy – Vivid and gripping novel telling the story of California's surfers by Kevin McAleer, published in 2007

Aviator – Leonardo DiCaprio plays the eccentric aviation pioneer and billionaire Howard Hughes in this 2005 film depicting a piece of Californian history

LA Confidential – Thriller by James Ellroy from the heart of the corrupt scene of police and politics in the L.A. of the 1940s, made into a movie with Russell Crowe and Kim Basinger (1997)

Chinatown – Roman Polanski's 1974 classic, where Jack Nicholson plays a private eye investigating a water scandal in Owens Valley

Sideways – Oscar-winning charming film about American wine culture (2005), using the vineyard country around Santa Barbara as the backdrop. In Santa Ynez Valley, a real cult has grown up around pinot noir. Two disappointed men in their mid-forties attempt to emulate the lifestyle of wine connoisseurs (2004)

ELECTRICITY

110 volts/60 hertz. While small appliances (electric shavers, hairdryers) will also work with this voltage, you'll need a three-pin to US two-pin adapter for the socket.

EMERGENCY

911 is the central number for police and health emergencies.

GETTING AROUND BY PUBLIC TRANSPORT

The railway company *Amtrak* offers a *California Rail Pass (www.amtrak.com) valid for 7–21 days. Greyhound (www.greyhound.com)* is the overland bus company with the best network. For more information, speak to travel agents.

HEALTH

The emergency departments at hospitals, well signalled outside as *Emergency Room*, help with acute emergency situations. Usually staff will ask for a credit card (generally Mastercard or Visa) before starting the treatment. Whatever you do, arrive with a travel health insurance policy.

INFORMATION

CALIFORNIA TOURISM

You can order a collection of brochures containing maps and other information via email at *infopaket@visitcalifornia.de*.
The following web sites also provide excellent detailed information:
– *www.visittheusa.com*
– *www.visittheusa.com*
– *www.parks.ca.gov*
Even in smaller towns, *Visitor Centers*

BUDGETING

Soft drink	£0.90–2.20/$1.20–2.90 *for 1 bottle of coke*
Beer	£3.50–5.30/$4.60–7 *for 1 glass in a bar*
Burger	£3.50/$4.60 *for a giant burger at In-N-Out*
Jeans	£30–44/$40–58 *for a pair of Levi's*
Petrol	£2.60/$3.50 *for 1 gallon (3.78 l) unleaded*
Taxi	£1.80–2.20/$2.30–2.90 *per mile (1.6 km)*

have information available on the region. For visitors arriving by car, well-equipped *Welcome Centers* in the big cities and near the state borders are good sources of information. *www.visitcwc.com*

INTERNET & WIFI

As the birthplace of the internet, California is perfectly connected. Where there's no free wireless provision, internet access in hotels usually costs $8–15 per day, but there's often a computer in the hotel lobby that is free to use. For your own laptop or netbook you'll find WiFi access is available in many hotels and cafés, sometimes free, sometimes on payment of a charge. For $2–3 per 10 minutes to check your mails, web access is available in coffee shops or office services such as *Kinko's*.

IMMIGRATION

For trips of up to three months, British and Irish travellers don't require a visa.

What is required is the machine-readable passport with biometric data. Note that new children's passports require a visa, so it's best to request a regular passport straight away! Before the trip, any visitor without a visa has to register online, incurring a fee payable by credit card *(https://esta.cbp.dhs.gov and www.dhs. gov | $14)*. This registration is then valid for two years for any follow-up trip. Further information: *www.dhs.gov*

MONEY

Pounds or euros in cash can only be changed at airports and in major hotels; even US banks (open on weekdays 10am–3pm) don't usually offer any changing services. The most popular means of payment are credit cards (Visa and Mastercard being the most common, ironically American Express much less so!). You'll get cash using your debit/credit card and four-digit PIN at most ATMs/cash machines, but you might want to let your bank or credit card company know you're travelling and ascertain your limit. Travellers cheques are accepted everywhere – your change will be in cash.

1 dollar = 100 cents. *Bills* (notes) are available in the denominations of 1, 5, 10, 20, 100 dollars. *Coins* are available in denominations of: *penny* (1 cent), *nickel* (5 cent), *dime* (10 cent), *quarter* (25 cent), *buck* (1 dollar).

NUDIST BATHING

In prudish America, public displays of nudity are prohibited. There are only a few privately run nudist beaches.

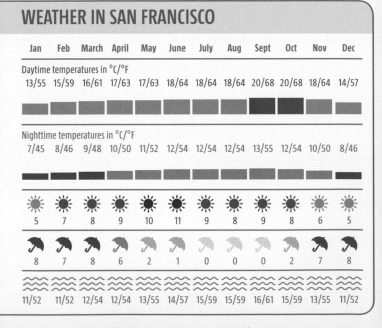

WEATHER IN SAN FRANCISCO

	Jan	Feb	March	April	May	June	July	Aug	Sept	Oct	Nov	Dec
Daytime temperatures in °C/°F	13/55	15/59	16/61	17/63	17/63	18/64	18/64	18/64	20/68	20/68	18/64	14/57
Nighttime temperatures in °C/°F	7/45	8/46	9/48	10/50	11/52	12/54	12/54	12/54	13/55	12/54	10/50	8/46
Sunshine hours/day	5	7	8	9	10	11	9	8	9	8	6	5
Precipitation days/month	8	7	8	6	2	1	0	0	0	2	7	8
Water temperature in °C/°F	11/52	11/52	12/54	12/54	13/55	14/57	15/59	15/59	16/61	15/59	13/55	11/52

PHONE & MOBILE PHONE

For long-distance calls within the US: dial the digit 1 before the three-digit *area code*. The operator (dial 0) helps with establishing a *collect call* (only within the US) and with questions. All numbers starting with 1 800, 1 844, 1 888, 1 866 and 1 877 are toll-free. Rental car firms, airlines and hotel chains offer this service for reservations.

To reach the UK from the US, dial 01144, followed by the area code without the 0. Calling from public phone boxes costs between 25 and 50 cents. Many hotels charge $2 or more for a unit. Tri and quad-band mobiles also work in California for a roaming surcharge of up to 1.70 pounds per minute. A cheaper option for calls from phone boxes and hotels are *prepaid phone cards* available from petrol stations and grocery stores.

POST

Most post offices are open Mon–Fri 9am–5pm, some also Sat 9am–midday. Stamps are also available from *drugstores*. Postage for air-mail letters or postcards to Europe is $1.15.

TAX

Depending on the region, sales tax in California varies between 7.5 and 10 per cent. Careful: sales tax is only added at the till, so doesn't appear on menus or price tags. Some hotel add an overnight accommodation tax of a few per cent.

TIME

Pacific Standard Time (PST): Greenwich Mean Time (GMT) minus eight hours. Summer time runs from mid-March to early November.

TIPPING

Restaurant prices don't include the service charge, so waiters receive 15–20 per cent of the end price *as a tip*. In hotels, luggage porters *(bell boys)* expect at least $1 per item. And don't forget the chambermaid!

WEIGHTS & MEASUREMENTS

1 inch = 2.54 cm
1 foot = 30.48 cm
1 yard = 91.44 cm
1 mile = 1.6 km
1 pint = 0.47 litres
1 gallon = 3.79 litres
1 pound = 453.6 g

To convert temperatures: Fahrenheit minus 32 x 5 divided by 9 gives you Celsius: 0 °C = 32 °F, 10 °C = 50 °F, 20 °C = 68 °F, 30 °C = 86 °F, 40 °C = 104 °F

Clothes sizes: for women, US size 4 is equivalent to the British 8, 6 = 10, 8 = 12, 10 = 14, 12 = 16, 14 = 18. For men, US size: 38 = 34, 39 = 36, 40 = 38, 41 = 40, 42 = 42, 43 = 44, 44 = 46, 45 = 48

ROAD ATLAS

The green line indicates the Discovery Tour "California at a glance"
The blue line indicates the other Discovery Tours

All tours are also marked on the pull-out map

Photo: Golden Gate Bridge, San Francisco

Exploring California

The map on the back cover shows how
the area has been sub-divided

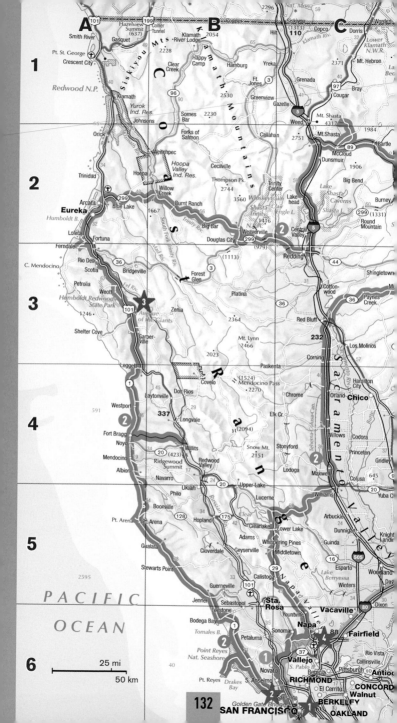

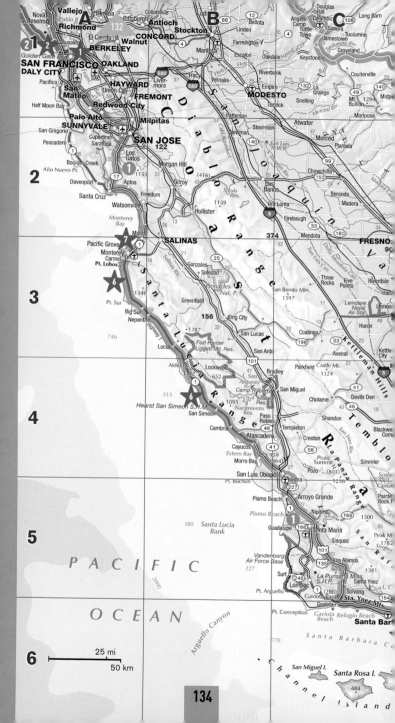

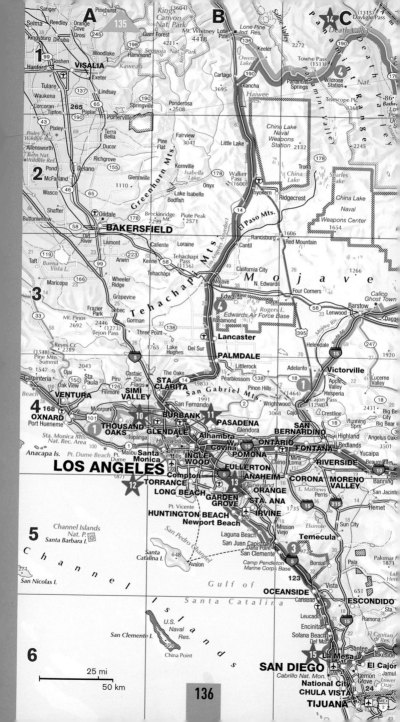

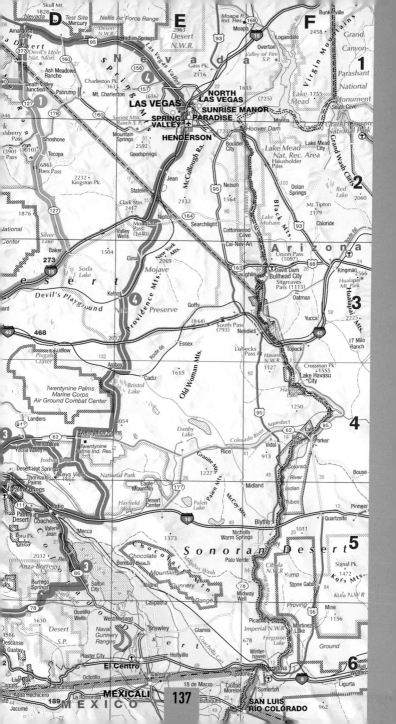

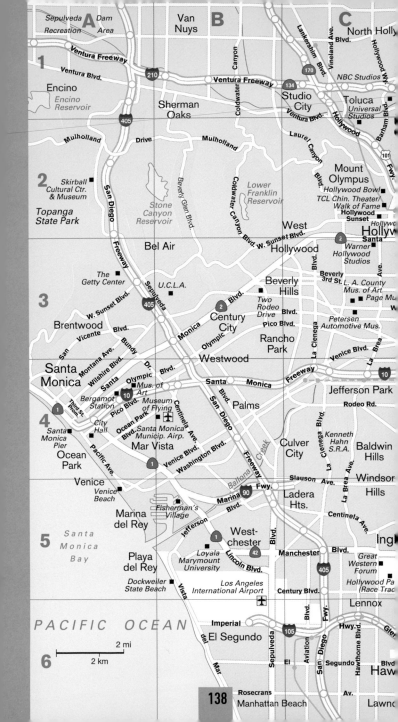

KEY TO ROAD ATLAS

Autobahn, mehrspurige Straße - in Bau Highway, multilane divided road - under construction	═══ ═ ═ ═	Autoroute, route à plusieurs voies - en construction Autopista, carretera de más carriles - en construcción
Fernverkehrsstraße - in Bau Trunk road - under construction	━━━ ━ ━ ━	Route à grande circulation - en construction Ruta de larga distancia - en construcción
Hauptstraße Principal highway	──────	Route principale Carretera principal
Nebenstraße Secondary road	──────	Route secondaire Carretera secundaria
Fahrweg, Piste Practicable road, track	──────	Chemin carrossable, piste Camino vecinal, pista
Straßennummerierung Road numbering	① **48** ⟨1⟩ ㉖ **26**	Numérotage des routes Numeración de carreteras
Entfernungen in mi. (USA), in km (MEX) Distances in mi. (USA), in km (MEX)	**259** 130 ╲ 129	Distances en mi. (USA), en km (MEX) Distancias en mi. (USA), en km (MEX)
Höhe in Meter - Pass Height in meters - Pass	1365 • ⌣	Altitude en mètres - Col Altura en metros - Puerto de montaña
Eisenbahn Railway	──────	Chemin-de-fer Ferrocarril
Autofähre - Schifffahrtslinie Car ferry - Shipping route	─ ─ ─ ─	Bac autos - Ligne maritime Transportador de automóviles - Ferrocarriles
Wichtiger internationaler Flughafen - Flughafen Major international airport - Airport	✈ ✈	Aéroport important international - Aéroport Aeropuerto importante internacional - Aeropuerto
Internationale Grenze - Bundesstaatengrenze International boundary - federal boundary	▨▨▨━▨▨	Frontière nationale - Frontière fédérale Frontera nacional - Frontera federal
Unbestimmte Grenze Undefined boundary	▨▨━▨▨━▨	Frontière d'État non définie Frontera indeterminada
Zeitzonengrenze Time zone boundary	-4h Greenwich Time ••••••••••• -3h Greenwich Time	Limite de fuseau horaire Límite del huso horario
Hauptstadt eines souveränen Staates National capital	**WASHINGTON**	Capitale nationale Capital de un estado soberano
Hauptstadt eines Bundesstaates State capital	**PHOENIX**	Capitale d'un état fédéral Capital de estado
Sperrgebiet Restricted area	▨▨▨▨▨	Zone interdite Zona prohibida
Indianerreservat - Nationalpark Indian reservation - National park	▨▨ ▨▨	Réserve d'indiens - Parc national Reserva de indios - Parque nacional
Sehenswertes Kulturdenkmal Interesting cultural monument	★ *Disneyland*	Monument culturel intéressant Monumento cultural de interés
Sehenswertes Naturdenkmal Interesting natural monument	✳ *Niagara Falls*	Monument naturel intéressant Monumento natural de interés
Brunnen, Salzsee Well, Salt lake	⌣ ▨	Puits, Lac salé Pozo, Lago salado
MARCO POLO Erlebnistour 1 MARCO POLO Discovery Tour 1	▬▬▬	MARCO POLO Tour d'aventure 1 MARCO POLO Recorrido aventura 1
MARCO POLO Erlebnistouren MARCO POLO Discovery Tours	▬▬▬	MARCO POLO Tours d'aventure MARCO POLO Recorridos de aventura
MARCO POLO Highlight	★	MARCO POLO Highlight

FOR YOUR NEXT TRIP...

MARCO POLO TRAVEL GUIDES

Algarve
Amsterdam
Andalucia
Athens
Australia
Austria
Bali & Lombok
Bangkok
Barcelona
Berlin
Brazil
Bruges
Brussels
Budapest
Bulgaria
California
Cambodia
Canada East
Canada West / Rockies
& Vancouver
Cape Town &
Garden Route
Cape Verde
Channel Islands
Chicago & The Lakes
China
Cologne
Copenhagen
Corfu
Costa Blanca
& Valencia
Costa Brava
Costa del Sol &
Granada
Costa Rica
Crete
Cuba
Cyprus (North and
South)
Devon & Cornwall
Dresden
Dubai

Dublin
Dubrovnik &
Dalmatian Coast
Edinburgh
Egypt
Egypt Red Sea Resorts
Finland
Florence
Florida
French Atlantic Coast
French Riviera
(Nice, Cannes & Monaco)
Fuerteventura
Gran Canaria
Greece
Hamburg
Hong Kong & Macau
Ibiza
Iceland
India
India South
Ireland
Israel
Istanbul
Italy
Japan
Jordan
Kos
Krakow
Lake District
Lake Garda
Lanzarote
Las Vegas
Lisbon
London
Los Angeles
Madeira & Porto Santo
Madrid
Maldives
Mallorca
Malta & Gozo
Mauritius

Menorca
Milan
Montenegro
Morocco
Munich
Naples & Amalfi Coast
New York
New Zealand
Norway
Oslo
Oxford
Paris
Peru & Bolivia
Phuket
Portugal
Prague
Rhodes
Rome
Salzburg
San Francisco
Santorini
Sardinia
Scotland
Seychelles
Shanghai
Sicily
Singapore
South Africa
Sri Lanka
Stockholm
Switzerland
Tenerife
Thailand
Tokyo
Turkey
Turkey South Coast
Tuscany
United Arab Emirates
USA Southwest
(Las Vegas, Colorado,
New Mexico, Arizona
& Utah)
Venice
Vienna
Vietnam
Zakynthos & Ithaca,
Kefalonia, Lefkas

INDEX

This index lists all places and destinations mentioned in the guide. Page numbers in bold type refer to the main entry.

Amboy 110
Anaheim 87
Anza Borrego Desert State Park 108
Auburn 59
Avenue of the Giants 45, 106
Baja California 99
Baker 103
Barstow 31, 103
Berkeley 27
Beverly Hills 23, 74, 76, 103
Big Sur 47, **60**
Blythe 90
Bodega Bay 55
Bodie **73**, 104
Cabazon 31, 109
Calico 103
Calistoga 52, 106
Carlsbad 108, 119
Carmel 57, **62**, 102, 119
Cascade Range 16, 49, 50
Channel Islands 24, **69**
Coachella Valley 108
Coloma 59
Colorado Desert 86
Colorado River Area 89
Columbia 58, 104
Coulterville 56
Crescent City 47
Dana Point **93**, 108
Dante's View 91
Death Valley 13, 17, 24, 87, **90**, 103, 111, 112
Disneyland 14, **88**, 103, 116
Edna Valley 67
Eureka **44**, 106
Ferndale **46**, 47, 106, 121
Fort Bragg 47, 49, 50, 106
Fort Ross State Historic Park 55, 105
Getty Center 78
Gold Country 30, 56, **58**, 104
Grass Valley 59
Gualala 55
Healdsburg 54
Hearst Castle 67
Henry Cowell State Park 102
Highway 1 16, 57, **60**, 103
Highway 49 58
Hollywood 15, **23**, 74, 81, 103
Hollywood Boulevard 78
Humboldt Redwoods State Park 45, 106
Huntington Beach **93**, 115, 121

Jamestown 58, 104
Jedediah Smith Redwoods State Park 47
Joshua Tree National Park 11, 17, 89, **95**, 109, 110
King Range National Conservation Area 47
Kings Canyon National Park 56, **70**
Knott's Berry Farm **89**, 116
Laguna Beach **92**, 107
Lake Havasu 22
Lake Havasu City 89
Lake Shasta 50
Lake Tahoe 56, **63**, 104, 115, 118, 120
Las Vegas 26, 103, 110, 111
Lassen Volcanic National Park 24, **48**, 106
Los Angeles 14, 16, 17, 21, 22, 23, 25, 30, **74**, 103, 107, 119, 120, 124, 144
Lost Coast 47, 106
Malakoff Diggins Historic State Park 59
Malibu 23, 74
Mammoth 73
Marina del Rey 74
Mendocino **49**, 50, 106, 119
Modesto 126
Mojave Desert 86
Mojave National Preserve **91**, 110
Mono Lake 56, **73**, 103
Montana de Oro State Park 67
Monterey **62**, 102, 118, 121
Monterey Peninsula 62
Morro Bay State Park 67
Morro Rock 67
Mount Shasta 16, **50**, 106, 114
Mount Tamalpais 112
Muir Woods **42**, 113
Napa (town) 52, 106
Napa Valley 29, 44, **52**, 104, 106
Needles 89
Nepenthe 61
Nevada City 58, 59
Newport Beach 93, 107, 121
Oakhurst 58
Oakville 52
Pacific Grove 102
Pacific Palisades 74
Palm Springs 17, 24, 87, **93**, 109, 113

Pasadena **85**, 120
Patrick's Point State Park 48
Pebble Beach 62, 113
Pfeiffer Big Sur State Park 60
Pinnacles National Park 24
Placerville 58
Point Lobos State Reserve 63
Point Reyes National Seashore **54**, 105, 119
Prairie Creek Redwoods State Park 47
Redding **52**, 106
Redwood National Park 24, **47**
Richardson Grove State Park 45
Rutherford 52
Sacramento 56, 60, **64**, 104, 120
Sacramento Valley 25
Salinas 63
San Diego 14, 22, 24, 30, 86, **95**, 108, 120
San Francisco 16, 18, 19, 22, 24, 25, 27, 30, **32**, 101, 106, 112, 113, 115, 117, 120, 124, 128, 144
San Juan Capistrano **93**, 108
San Luis Obispo 57, **66**, 67, 103
San Simeon 57, 67
Santa Barbara 30, 57, **68**, 103, 115, 119, 121, 126
Santa Catalina Island 85
Santa Clara Valley 43
Santa Cruz 101, 119
Santa Monica 30, 74, **80**, 103
Santa Ynez Valley 69
Sausalito **43**, 121
Scotty's Castle 90
Sea World 96
Sequoia National Park 24, 56, **70**
Shasta Cascade 51
Sierra Nevada 13, 22, 71
Silicon Valley **43**, 101
Sinkyone Wilderness State Park 47
Skunk Train 49, 106
Solvang 69
Sonoma 54, 106
Sonoma Coast **55**, 105
Sonoma Valley 29, **54**
Squaw Valley 64
Sutter Creek 58
Sutter's Fort State Historic Park 65

CREDITS

The Living Desert **94**, 109
Tiburon 43
Tijuana 99
Trees of Mystery 47
Trinidad 45, **48**

Universal Studios **80**, 103, 116
Vacaville 31
Venice Beach 74, **80**, 144
Weaverville 106
Willits 106

Yosemite National Park 14, 15, 24, 56, **71**, 104, 114
Yosemite Valley 71
Yountville 52

WRITE TO US

e-mail: info@marcopologuides.co.uk
Did you have a great holiday?
Is there something on your mind?
Whatever it is, let us know!
Whether you want to praise, alert us
to errors or give us a personal tip –
MARCO POLO would be pleased to
hear from you.
We do everything we can to provide the
very latest information for your trip.

Nevertheless, despite all of our authors'
thorough research, errors can creep in.
MARCO POLO does not accept any
liability for this. Please contact us by
e-mail or post.
MARCO POLO Travel Publishing Ltd
Pinewood, Chineham Business Park
Crockford Lane, Chineham
Basingstoke, Hampshire RG24 8AL
United Kingdom

PICTURE CREDITS
Cover Photograph: Santa Monica, beach (gettyimages: E. Davies)
Photos: 111 Minna Gallery: Daniel Kokin (19 bottom); AW L Images: D. Delimont (17, 95), T. Mackie (20/21), S. Po-
liti Markovina (76/77), M. Simoni (97); W. Dieterich (30, 48, 61, 66, 69, 123); DuMont Bildarchiv: Heeb (6, 31,
46, 56/57), Piepenburg (28 left, 55); gettyimages: E. Davies (1); huber-images: C. Dutton (52), Eisele-Hein (110),
Kremer (74/75, 83), S. Kremer (12/13), T. Mackie (100/101), S. Parisi (80), Ripani (72), Giovanni Simeone (flap
left, 34, 112/113), R. Spila (11); © iStockphoto: Sibel A. Roberts (18 bottom), Polina Yun (19 top); Laif: Heeb (107),
Modrow (41); Laif/A urora (122 top, Benson (7); Laif/hemis.fr (98); Laif/Redux: Flores (85); mauritius images:
Kinne (14/15), Schön (86/87), Vidler (88, 120), Weber (30/31); mauritius images/age (22, 134/135); mauritius images/Alamy (2, 3, 5, 29, 43, 44/45, 51, 58, 65, 90, 92, 105, 114, 116/117, 118, 120/121, 121), R. Bishop (25),
A. Pierce (62); mauritius images/A lamy/eye35.pix (4 top, 32/33); mauritius images/A lamy/McPhoto: Lovell
(37); mauritius images/FreshFood (26/27); mauritius images/Image Source: B. Stevens (18 top); mauritius ima-
ges/imagebroker: Rudi Sebastian (9), Siebert (70); mauritius images/Robert Harding (79); Adrienne Nunez (18
centre); Schapowalow/SI ME: M. Rellini (38), M. Ripani (4 bottom); T. Stankiewicz (flap right, 8, 10, 122
bottom); varioimages/Design Pics (28 right)

3rd edition – fully revised and updated 2020
Worldwide Distribution: Marco Polo Travel Publishing Ltd, Pinewood, Chineham Business Park, Crockford Lane,
Basingstoke, Hampshire RG24 8AL, United Kingdom. Email: sales@marcopoloUk.com
© MAIRDUMONT GmbH & Co. KG, Ostfildern
Chief editor: Stefanie Penck
Author: Karl Teuschl, editor: Marlis v. Hessert-Fraatz
Programme supervision: Lucas Forst-Gill, Susanne Heimburger, Johanna Jiranek, Nikolai Michaelis, Kristin
Wittemann, Tim Wohlbold
Picture editors: Gabriele Forst
What's hot: Karl Teuschl, wunder media, Munich
Cartography road atlas and pull-out map: © MAIRDUMONT, Ostfildern
Cover design, p. 1, pull-out map cover: Karl Anders – Büro für Visual Stories, Hamburg; design inside:
milchhof:atelier, Berlin; design p. 2/3, Discovery Tours: Susan Chaaban Dipl. Des. (FH)
Translated from German by Kathleen Becker, Jennifer Walcoff Neuheiser and Lindsay Chalmers-Gerbracht
Editorial office: SAW Communications, Redaktionsbüro Dr. Sabine A. Werner, Mainz: Julia Gilcher, Cosima Talhouni,
Dr. Sabine A. Werner, Sarah Wirth; prepress: SAW Communications, Mainz, in cooperation with alles mit Medien, Mainz
Phrase book in cooperation with Ernst Klett Sprachen GmbH, Stuttgart, Edi-
torial by PONS Wörterbücher

MIX
Paper from
responsible sources
FSC® C124385

DOS & DON'TS 👍

Last but not least, here are a few things that you should avoid

UNDERESTIMATING IMPORTANT ISSUES

Too much sun can easily spoil the holiday fun. Be particularly careful in the Sierra Nevada where many trails are 3,000 m/9,843 ft above sea level, and even more so in the burning heat of Death Valley. It also helps to schedule estimated arrival times etc. if you bear in mind that traffic in America flows more slowly than you might be used to.

GIVING IN TO THE JETLAG

The human body compensates the time difference of eight hours between the British Isles and California (less for travellers within the US) within two or three days. After arrival try and fight the inevitable tiredness with a walk in some fresh air, and only head for bed around 9pm. Long-haul travel pros drink large amounts of mineral water for prevention purposes.

UNDERESTIMATING THE TRAFFIC

Avoid any Los Angeles freeway between 8 and 10am and between 4 and 6pm when the highways are one huge traffic jam. Also don't schedule your trip to Malibu for a foggy day, or go cruising on Mulholland Drive above Hollywood when there's smog.

TAKING UNNECESSARY RISKS

At night, try to avoid the neighbourhoods known to be hotspots of crime (Los Angeles: South Central L.A., Watts, parts of West Hollywood and Venice Beach; San Francisco: all parks and the Tenderloin quarter).

LEAVING HIKING TRAILS

Remember that it's very easy to get lost in the great outdoors. Stay on the signposted trails, and don't forget to leave your names, the time you started the hike and an ETA at the trailhead when making longer excursions into the wilderness. This enables the local rangers to go and look for you if you haven't returned from the wilderness in time.

LEAVING YOUR PASSPORT AT THE HOTEL

Not because it might get stolen there, but because you'll often need the document: it might be the lady at the desk where you cash in your travellers cheques, the barman, or the guy selling you cigarettes or alcohol at the petrol station. ID is essential.

DRINKING ALCOHOL IN PUBLIC

In the US, it's forbidden to drink in the street – alcohol must be wrapped (usually in a brown paper bag). Drivers should not drink any alcohol. If there's an accident, the insurance won't pay, and the rental car company might deduct the value of the entire car from your credit card!

Thinking Reasonably

Reaching Emotional Peace
Through Mental Toughness

Dale R. Olen, Ph.D.

A Life Skills Series Book

JODA Communications, Ltd.
Milwaukee, Wisconsin

Editor: Carolyn Kott Washburne
Design: Chris Roerden and Associates
Layout: Eileen Olen

Copyright 1993 by Dale R. Olen, Ph.D.

ISBN 1-56583-004-0

Published by: JODA Communications, Ltd.
10125 West North Avenue
Milwaukee, WI 53226

PRINTED IN THE UNITED STATES OF AMERICA

Table of Contents

		page
Introduction to the Life Skills Series		5
Chapter One:	What Is the Skill of Thinking Reasonably?	9
Chapter Two:	Principles and Tools for Thinking Reasonably	15
Chapter Three:	Beliefs that Lead to Peace of Mind	39
Chapter Four:	Developing this Skill with Others	55
Appendix:	Review of Principles for Thinking Reasonably	59

Introduction
to the
Life Skills Series

Nobody gets out alive! It isn't easy navigating your way through life. Your relationships, parents, marriage, children, job, school, church, all make big demands on you. Sometimes you feel rather ill-equipped to make this journey. You feel as if you have been tossed out in the cold without even a warm jacket. Life's journey demands considerable skill. Navigating the sometimes smooth, other times treacherous journey calls for a wide variety of tools and talents. When the ride feels like a sailboat pushed by a gentle breeze, slicing through the still waters, you go with the flow. You live naturally with the skills already developed.

But other times (and these other times can make you forget the smooth sailing), the sea turns. The boat shifts violently, driven by the waves' force. At those stormy moments, you look at your personal resources, and they just don't seem sufficient.

Gabriel Marcel, the French philosopher, wrote that the journey of life is like a spiral. The Greeks, he observed, viewed life as *cyclical*—sort of the same old thing over and over. The seasons came, went, and came again. History repeated itself. The Hebrews, on the other hand, saw life as *linear*—a pretty straight march toward a goal. You begin at the Alpha point and end at Omega. It's as simple as that.

Marcel combined the two views by capturing the goal-oriented optimism of the Hebrews and the sobering reality of the Greeks' cycles. Life has its ups and downs, but it always moves forward.

To minimize the *downs* and to make the most of the *ups*, you need **Life Skills**. When you hike down the Grand Canyon, you use particular muscles in your back and legs. And when you trudge up the Canyon, you use other muscles. So too with life skills. You call on certain skills when your life spirals down, such as the skill of defeating depression and managing stress. When your life is on an upswing, you employ skills like thinking reasonably and meeting life head on.

This series of books is about the skills you need for getting through life. To get from beginning to end without falling flat on your face and to achieve some dignity and some self-satisfaction, you need **basic** life skills. These include:

1. Accepting yourself.
2. Thinking reasonably.
3. Meeting life head on.

With these three life skills mastered to some degree, you can get a handle on your life. Now, if you want to build from there, you are going to need a few more skills. These include:

4. Communicating.
5. Managing stress.
6. Being intimate.
7. Resolving conflict.
8. Reducing anger.
9. Overcoming fear.
10. Defeating depression.

If you have these ten skills up and running in your life, you are ready to face yourself, your relationships, your parents, your marriage, your children, your job and even God with the hope of handling whatever comes your way. Without these skills, you are going to bump into one stone wall after another. These skills don't take away the problems, the challenges and the hard times. But they do help you dig out of life's deep trenches and more fully *enjoy* the good times.

Life Skills can be learned. You have what it takes to master each of these skills–even if you feel you don't have the tiniest bit of the skill right now. But nobody can develop the skill for you. You have to take charge and develop it yourself. Your family, friends and community may be able to help you, but you are the center at which each skill has to start. Here is all you need to begin this learning process:

- Awareness.
- The desire to grow.
- Effort and practice.

Awareness begins the process of change. You have to notice yourself, watch your behavior and honestly face your strengths and weaknesses. You have to take stock of each skill and of the obstacles in you that might inhibit its growth.

Once you recognize the value of a skill and focus on it, you have to want to pursue it. The critical principle here, one you will see throughout this series, is *desire*. Your desire will force you to focus on the growing you want to do and keep you going when learning comes hard.

Finally, your *effort and practice* will make these **Life Skills** come alive for you. You can do it. The ten books in the **Life Skills Series** are tools to guide and encourage your progress. They are my way of being with you–cheering your efforts. But without your practice, what you find in these books will wash out to sea.

Working on these ten **Life Skills** won't get you through life without any scars. But the effort you put in will help you measure your life in more than years. Your life will be measured in the zest, faith, love, honesty and generosity you bring to yourself and your relationships.

I can hardly wait for you to get started!

Chapter One

What Is the Skill of Thinking Reasonably?

Back in 1980 I bought a Mercury LN7, a poor man's sports car. It was a nifty little orange job that made a lot of noise but didn't go fast. My son, Andy, was five at the time. He announced to me from the back seat one day that this car had speakers in the back as well as in the front. I said paternalistically, "No, Andy, this car only has speakers in the front." He disagreed, but of course to no avail. I knew.

Over the next couple of years he tried several more times to convince me there were speakers in the back. I tried patiently to explain that it only seemed that way, because the sound from the front speakers was probably wrapping around the windows and hitting him from behind. Logical explanation. Actually almost insightful if you ask me.

Then came the day of my enlightenment. Almost three years from the time Andy first informed me about the back speakers, I was cleaning the rear window from the inside. The radio was on. And lo and behold, there were, in fact, two speakers in the back of that car.

There couldn't be, I thought. I remember reading in the owner's manual that this car had only two front speakers. But I couldn't deny the fact. Andy was right. What I thought to be true was false. My perception of reality did not, in fact, match reality. I sat in the back seat of that car staring blankly into space. Could there possibly be other areas in my life where what I thought to be true was not so?

Copernicus came to mind. Andy probably felt in a small way what Copernicus must have experienced on a grander scale. Everyone believed the sun went around the earth. It certainly appeared that way. Copernicus came along and said no. It was just the opposite. "Sure, sure, Coper," must have been the response. Gradually, the facts came in and people could no longer deny them. By golly, Copernicus was right. People's perception and judgment about reality had been incorrect all this time.

Have you ever had a Copernicus experience? Or an LN7 experience? If so, you know the need to develop the *skill of thinking reasonably*. You realize that *what* you think, and at times *how* you think, may be somewhat left or right of center (and I'm not talking politics here). Your thoughts have not always accurately reflected reality. You may have failed to hear what someone actually said. You heard it but embellished it with your own dressing. You may have dramatized it, blowing it out of all proportion. If you're like me, at times you have even distorted some information in order to fit it into your own rigid view of the world. Unfortunately, it's very difficult for us to recognize our own unreasonable thinking.

As I began writing about the skill of thinking reasonably, I wondered if anyone would ever actually read this book. "I don't need this. If there is one skill I have, it's thinking reasonably." I figured most people who picked up this book would be thinking of someone they could give it to – the people who *really* need it. It could be a best seller. Nobody would ever read it, but it would get passed on from friend to acquaintance. People would think: "This would be a very good book for George to read." George would receive the book and say, "I don't need this, but Karen ought to read this," and pass it on to her. It's easy to spot unreasonable thinking in your friends and relatives, but harder to notice it in yourself. I encourage you to pay attention first to the irrational thoughts within yourself.

Personal conflict offers one of the best opportunities to observe your unreasonable thinking. A colleague points out an inconsistency in a report you wrote. He says, "Jim, that report doesn't make much sense. I didn't understand it." Your thinking process begins. You go right for his jugular. "What a jerk. He is forever criticizing me and others. He must feel inadequate, having to put the rest of us down in order to look good himself."

You might then turn your runaway mind on yourself: "I never do anything right. I'm just not as good as the others. I should probably look for some other kind of work. I'll never be successful here." You can even take a few shots at the boss: "She always gives me the hard projects. I don't think she likes me anyway. Probably wants to drive me out of here. She's so into power. I hate this job."

In the passion of the moment, these thoughts seem perfectly reasonable to you. But when you see them written out on a page like this, you can step back and say, "Well, sure. Those are very strong statements. I don't think like that." Oh yeah! Wanna bet?

Certainly you and I observe unreasonable thinking going on all around us. Unfortunately, much of it we simply accept:

- World leaders resolve geographical and power issues by having young boys kill each other in wars.
- Car dealers try selling cars by draping women across the hoods.
- Black people, brown people, red people, women and old people are often discriminated against simply because they appear different.
- More and more people physically strike out against those they love as a way of resolving conflict.
- Alcohol and drugs act as solutions to life's problems.

Well, you get the idea. We are immersed in irrational thinking. Because it's so present, it becomes easy to forget how unreasonable all these responses are. Also, because you and I are so used to and comfortable with ourselves, we become blind to our own nonsensical thinking. Maybe the rest of the world is crazy, but you and I, at least, have our acts together. Well, I know I do. But I'm not always so sure about you!

The skill of thinking reasonably will make sense to you only when you're willing to throw a little doubt into your beliefs. In fact, you do not always think reasonably. You – like most people – make many mistakes in perceiving and judging reality. At times you live near the edge of reality in the way you think.

How can you know your thinking is unreasonable? You know it by the impact your thinking has on your emotions and behaviors. If you live with emotions that continually sabotage your happiness, you are thinking irrationally. If you behave in ways that interfere with your personal relationships or with the productive use of your time, then you know your thinking is out of touch with reality. If you keep having the same problem and continue trying to solve it by "doing more of the same," then you know something is the matter with your thinking.

Your thoughts create your feelings and your behaviors. You *think,* for example, "I want to learn this skill of reasonable thinking. To do so, I will sit down and read this book." That thought process produces your present behavior. Simple enough, right? You spot a little leak in the kitchen sink faucet. You think to yourself, "I ought to fix that right away before it gets any bigger. But I really want to finish this novel. I have worked hard all day and deserve a break." So you remain sitting and read your book. You let the water faucet go. Your thinking is determining your behavior or lack of it.

Your thinking, then, plays the central role in creating emotions and behaviors. If your behaviors and feelings seem comfortable for you, if they work for your good and the good of others, then you can assume your thinking is quite reasonable. On the other hand, if your feelings and behaviors get you into trouble with yourself or with others, you can assume the culprit is your thinking – your beliefs, attitudes, conclusions and perceptions.

Thinking is to your psychological well-being what a strong heart is to your body's health. The *skill of thinking reasonably* stands as one of the three foundational skills upon which all other human skills grow. Along with the skills of *accepting yourself* and *meeting life head on, thinking reasonably* sets the stage for a full, happy and productive life. Thinking reasonably means seeing what's actually there. If you could videotape your next disagreement with a friend, you would understand this point. A videotape sees and hears what actually goes on. Matching that against your own mental view can be quite revealing. Suppose you're talking with your friend and make a hand gesture while listening to what he has to say. You think you're trying to be understanding. But when you watch the video replay, you see that your gesture looks more like a sign of disagreement than of understanding. You view yourself as a good listener, but the video picked up the waved hand and the deep sigh of disapproval you made. Making sure your view is like a videotape helps you think reasonably.

Reasonable thinking also involves the *conclusions* you draw once you have viewed reality. Do your conclusions flow out of the information you have? Or do they seem to jump steps?

For example, young people show unreasonable thinking when they begin smoking and don't think they will have a problem quitting. I had a 15-year-old boy tell me, "I smoke about a half a pack a day. I know it's bad for my health. But I decided I will quit when I'm 18. Smoking for three or four years won't bother me." My reaction was, "What? Did I miss something here?" Adults who just try cocaine "to see what it's like" show the same nonsensical thinking. Any time you and I draw conclusions that don't fit the facts, we demonstrate the lack of this skill.

More positively, reasonable thinking means stopping at the amber light in the busy intersection. It means talking directly to the person you have a problem with instead of ignoring her. It means getting the school or work assignment done on time. It means calling home if you will be later than expected. Emotionally it involves liking yourself even when you do make a mistake. It includes feeling happy at a friend's success instead of jealous; responding to the positive parts of life instead of focusing on the negative; spending more time living in the present than regretting the past or worrying about the future. Thus reasonable, sensible thinking includes getting the video camera out and paying attention to what is really out there – just the facts. Once you have the facts, reasonable thinking means drawing conclusions that protect you from unnecessary harm and lead you to happiness in your work and relationships. Reasonable thinking frees you from heavy and dark emotions. It brings you to peace, joy, contentment and a sense of well-being.

Chapter Two

Principles and Tools for Thinking Reasonably

N ow let's get to the mechanics of reasonable thinking. This skill takes considerable work. It's not easy to change beliefs and attitudes that have been your companions for years. So I encourage you to roll up your sleeves and dig into this powerful skill.

Principle 1

Your thoughts and beliefs create your feelings and behaviors.

This first principle helps you understand the dynamics of your thinking process. Most people don't believe this first principle. "What do you mean, I create my own feelings? Flying makes me nervous, the home team losing makes me sad and my kids make me angry." It sounds correct. The cause of your feelings seems to be outside of yourself. But what sounds right is, in fact, dead wrong.

Your feelings and your behaviors are not caused by other people or by circumstances outside of you. They are caused by your own thinking process. Certainly you need those other people and situations to trigger your thoughts, but it remains your thoughts that drive your feelings and behaviors.

You wouldn't get angry with the kids if they weren't fighting with each other. Right. You need the event to begin the process leading to your anger. Cognitive psychologists call these situations "Activating events." They kick your thinking systems into gear. Your thinking process then works so quickly that the next thing you experience is your emotional response. The kids fight, and you immediately respond with anger. It feels like a clean cause and effect relationship. The kids' misbehavior leads to your anger.

But something else is going on. In between the kids fighting and your responding with anger operates the real villain – your automatic thoughts. Most of these thoughts lie deep within you. They no longer need to be conscious. They simply roam around your unconscious mind, framing your responses to life's situations. It is these subtle beliefs – long held and cherished – that cause your emotional and behavioral responses.

For example, when I give talks to groups, I often ask for a volunteer to help me demonstrate something. As soon as I ask, I sense an emotional response on the part of many in the audience. Some people flush. Others look away. Still others get busy writing notes. Others calmly remain looking at me. Finally, one or two raise a hand to volunteer.

What happened to this audience? Did I cause many of them to become nervous? If I had that kind of power, why didn't everyone in the room respond with anxiety? If the cause of anxiety was my asking for a volunteer, then everyone's response should have been the same. But it wasn't. So something else was intervening, causing anxiety in some and willingness in others.

Albert Ellis, one of the first psychologists to show the

connection between thinking and feeling, developed a little outline that will help you understand the process of reasonable and unreasonable thinking. It goes like this:

A. Activating Event: Dale asking for a volunteer.
B. Beliefs: The audience's beliefs that led to anxiety.
   Examples of such beliefs include:
   "I don't know what he wants. I might not do it right."
   "I may make a fool out of myself."
   "He will make me say things I don't want to say."
   It is these beliefs that cause certain people to become nervous. The nervous reaction wasn't caused by my asking for the volunteer.
C. Consequences: People respond with anxiety, look away and don't raise their hands.

This process is called the ABCs of reasonable thinking. Beliefs about an event create emotions and behaviors. The conclusion to this?

Principle 2

**You are the cause of your feelings and behaviors.
Therefore, you have the power to change them.**

Listen to Frank, an alcoholic, who has been drinking for 11 years: "I hate this habit. I wish I could quit. But it's bigger than me. It runs my life. I have no control over the drinking. I feel powerless to stop it. I'll probably be this way all my life."

Frank experiences his drinking as something caused from outside himself. Because he does, he has no power to control it. He is, in effect, a victim of the alcohol demon. Liquor dominates him, not the other way around. What an awful predicament to be in. It feels much like the homeowner in a coastal town attempting to prepare for Hurricane Hugo. He has no control over the wind force. He feels helpless. The same is true for the earthquake victim. The earth moves from under her feet. She cannot stop the jolt. She is powerless.

You may feel like that with some of your emotions and behaviors. Maybe you have wanted to stop smoking for a long time. Every time you make the effort, you fail. Stopping smoking seems beyond your control. Or you say, "I am forever making resolutions to cut down on sugar, and I am forever breaking those resolutions. At those points I feel powerless in the face of sugar."

You might experience a lack of control with your anger or your fears or sorrows. For example, no matter how patient you try to be with the kids, you lose control after only two minutes. Without thinking about it much, you tend to think all your responses occur because of forces outside yourself. I'd like to invite you to turn that view upside down and recognize this most important belief: *You create your own feelings and behaviors. Therefore you have the power to change those you don't like.*

With this belief you become the master of your own destiny. You take charge of your behavior and your feelings. If there are certain emotional or behavioral responses you don't like, you then have the ability and power to change them. They are not out of your control. You do not want to give your power away. You can control your anger or worry. You can moderate your eating habits and discipline yourself to exercise three times a week.

With the focus on physical fitness these past years, you have probably gotten much better about taking charge of your body. You watch your cholesterol. You have cut back on desserts. You jog and swim and do aerobics. You have learned to believe that you can control your body to some degree. You have taken charge.

But when it comes to your mind, you may still be mentally flabby. You probably don't challenge your negative thinking. You may be giving away much of your mental power. You tend to regress to old beliefs that didn't work back then and still don't work now. But they are old friends. You feel comfortable with them, even though they don't work for you.

Just as you have realized you can take control of your body in significant ways, you need to win back the control of your mind. By altering the way you think, you change the way you feel and behave. Your anger is not caused by the car cutting in front of you. Your fear of heights cannot be blamed on the Hancock Building in Chicago. *You* make yourself angry. *You* cause yourself to worry. *You* keep yourself depressed. Because you do these things to yourself, you can take charge of your responses. As I will show you, you have the power to change!

Principle 3

Your old, automatic thoughts have the most influence on your feelings and behaviors.

At work, evaluation time approaches. Evaluations always bother you, even though you generally get good ratings. This time is no different. Your supervisor sounds pleased. The judgments seem positive, except for that one category – promptness. You receive "Needs improvement." You hit the ceiling. "What do you mean 'Needs improvement'?" you yell inside yourself. When you leave your supervisor's office, you flip-flop between anger and sadness. You forget all the positive comments your supervisor made, and you forget the nice raise you got for a job well done. All you can focus on is "Needs improvement."

If I ask you at the time, "What are you thinking that is making you angry and sad?" you might respond, "Nothing, other than she doesn't know what she's talking about." However, if we keep talking about your deeper, more automatic beliefs, you would eventually get in touch with some important thought patterns that kick in whenever a criticism appears.

These automatic and usually very old beliefs developed in childhood. We call them *personal constructs*. Personal constructs are beliefs and attitudes you formed very early in life by observing people and situations around you. In exploring your angry/sad response to the boss's criticism, you would probably find a powerful *construct* learned in childhood. That construct would be the culprit that created your anger and sadness over the criticism.

What could that construct be? Well, a few come to mind right away.

1. "If I don't do things perfectly, they are no good at all." This construct causes depression. It may have come from a parent who insisted on perfection. "B's are not satisfactory on your report card. You can do better."

2. "I am a good person only if you approve my work." Again, this belief leads to depression. Perhaps Mom or Dad taught you that you were acceptable only when you acted in "good" ways.

3. "It is unfair for people to criticize me, because they don't understand what I did." This is a typical child's belief that ends up in anger. Like many children you may have learned that if you didn't get your way or if people responded negatively to you, then you could claim "unfair." *Unfair* is one of those fightin' words and beliefs that leads to anger. If you feel you have been wronged, you want to fight back. Anger helps you do so.

These beliefs or constructs were developed by you as a child while you observed the interactions of people around you. You took in an awful lot of information back then. You put it into neat little packages and tucked it away in the basement of your subconscious mind. You concluded about all this information: "Oh, so that's the way I'm supposed to react and feel and behave." You learned your lessons well. Those constructs now sit in you as an adult. They dramatically influence your feelings and behavior. You no longer even need to be conscious of them. They know when to surface and influence you all on their own.

So as soon as the boss criticizes, those beliefs kick in. Without being aware of them, they cause your anger and sadness. You feel your anger/sadness and conclude that the boss caused those reactions in you. No. It was those old, automatic *constructs*.

Your anger was caused by the belief that no one should misunderstand you, and that the only reason you could be criticized would be because you were being misunderstood. You grow sad because you believe you have not lived up to others' expectations and thus have lost your boss's positive opinion of you.

What's incredible about *personal constructs* is their sticking power. In other words, once you have formed constructs, they tend to lock in. They sit in you like too much gummy oatmeal on a cold morning. Over the years of your life they don't want to budge, no matter what new information you might take in. Constructs become tight categories that imprison you from seeing in new and fresh ways.

In fact, if new information comes to you that contradicts your construct, you tend to reject the data. Perhaps you get down on yourself. You don't think you do anything well. Your friend compliments you on the committee work you did for the school bazaar. She tells you what a great job you did and how proud you should be of yourself. You pooh-pooh the compliment and internally hang onto the solid belief that you cannot do anything well.

On the other hand, imagine that the bazaar was not successful. Not many people showed up and the profit was low. No one says much of anything. You conclude, however, that this simply proves just how inadequate you are when it comes to doing these kinds of things.

When outside information supports your old construct of yourself, you accept the data without challenge. But when contradictory information comes in, you tend to dismiss the information and hold onto your construct. You cannot win – without hard work – when you have negative constructs.

Your old, automatic, negative beliefs, then, become your enemy. When you feel or behave in ways you don't like and you wish to change those responses, you need to look at the constructs you learned early in life. Those constructs need to be challenged and changed if you want to free yourself from feelings and behaviors that no longer work for you.

Principle 4

If you want to change your feelings or behaviors, then learn to *doubt* your beliefs or constructs.

I was a child in the 1940s. I learned what roles men and women should play in family life by watching my parents, grandparents, neighbors and relatives. I caught on fast that women should cook, clean the house, bake apple pies and cool them on the window sill. I figured out men should have at least two jobs (especially in tough times). They should come home from work and play roughhouse with the kids for a while. They should read the paper, cut the grass and repair the car.

I also was raised a Roman Catholic. So I learned it was wrong to go into a Lutheran church. I believed only Catholics could be "saved." I understood it was a sin to eat meat on Friday or miss church on Sunday. It was definitely not fitting to marry a non-Catholic.

Over the years my constructs about the roles of men and women and about religion have changed quite dramatically. What I once believed to be absolutely true no longer makes any sense. I still recall as a boy arguing passionately with my 10-year-old Lutheran friends about their need to join the Catholic church so they wouldn't go to hell when they died. Now I believe that my friends of all faiths, Christian or not, have the same opportunities regarding the next life–

if there is one. And I hope there is.

As a child I believed absolutely in a heaven and hell after life on earth. In fact, I figured we'd sit around all day in the clouds (maybe like living in Seattle) and eat bananas. As time has passed, I still *hope* there is a heaven, but I must admit doubt has raised its subtle question mark. And even if there is a heaven, I no longer wish it to be sitting in clouds eating bananas. My tastes have changed over the years.

You, too, can think of various "truths" you held as a child that have changed over time. When you were a youngster, you firmly believed sports figures could do no wrong. Now you know they too can succumb to alcohol, drugs and steroids. As a child you believed the United States government stood for justice and right at all times. Now you probably have doubts about its motives when you realize the power of the "military-industrial complex." When you were little you learned that eggs were good for you. Today you know they clog your arteries and cause heart disease.

You and I know, after having lived life for a while, that many things we held sacred, things we knew to be hard facts, have turned out to be at best merely opinions and at worst complete falsehoods. Many times, like the character played by Gilda Radnor on the television comedy, "Saturday Night Live," we have had to say, "Never mind."

When you realized your beliefs were changing, you probably responded in one of two different ways. Either:

1. "Darn it anyway. Why can't we have it one way and that's it? I hate when my beliefs have to keep changing. It confuses me and makes me upset. What's right is right; what's wrong is wrong. And it should stay that way. If something was true a hundred years ago, then it must be true today. So there."

Or:

2. "How exciting to live in a time of so much change! What

seemed real and true yesterday now is different because we have so much more information. It's challenging and wonderful to keep gaining new awareness and knowledge. My mind keeps growing and evolving every day. I can respect all I learned years ago as building blocks for what I understand today."

I hope you fall into this second category. I know I want to. It makes life so much more interesting to live. It gives you mental flexibility, which helps you deal more effectively with the information crunch and all the changes occurring every day.

I'm sure you have recognized changes in your beliefs over the years. Many of these changes you simply accepted. Some of them probably happened without your awareness. One day you realized your thinking on a certain subject had changed. What I'm discussing with you right now, though, are beliefs about external realities. New information about these issues causes you to seriously reconsider your position. Receiving satellite pictures of the earth from outer space clearly demonstrates that the earth is round – in case you may have been one of the last believers in the "flat world" theory. Hard data force you to change your beliefs.

But you have to contend with another set of beliefs that doesn't change so easily. These are the personal constructs you have formed about yourself and your relationships. The more personal your beliefs, the harder it is to change them. The more personal your constructs, the more you resist new information. At this personal level, I'm sorry to say, you tend to express the first response to change identified above: "Darn it anyway. If something was true 100 years ago (or 35 years ago), then it must still be true today. So there."

The constructs you learned about yourself early in childhood tend to get locked in. They are reinforced for you over the years. You likely hold these beliefs to be sacred. You have probably resisted allowing new information to penetrate these "laws of nature."

Some of the key personal beliefs I hear from clients include:

1. I am okay if I am successful. If I make the team, get good grades, get the promotion, have a sports car, have beautiful clothes, write a best seller, then I am okay.
2. Everything I do must be done perfectly. If I do something less than perfectly, it's no good. Doing things perfectly well ensures that others will respond positively to me. Then, and only then, can I feel good about myself.
3. I am okay if I please Daddy or Mommy. (This is often the root of beliefs 1 and 2 above.)
4. No matter what I do, it will never be good enough. Therefore, I am doomed to be miserable, since all I do will be considered a failure.
5. It's safer to keep quiet if I disagree. (This belief is often learned by children in alcoholic families.)
6. For all to be okay, things must be done in a certain way. That way is basically my way. I know the best way.
7. Other people should not make mistakes. (This, of course, causes anger when people do make mistakes.)
8. I shouldn't make any mistakes. (This causes guilt when I make the mistake.)
9. Others should amend their ways and ask forgiveness of me when they hurt me or violate my rules for them.

These are just a few examples of beliefs you might have that generally don't help you. Even though they sabotage your happiness and put you under a great deal of stress, they seem set in concrete. You don't like thinking this way. But you can't change the beliefs. Nonsense! You can change those old beliefs. If you can change all kind of external beliefs with new information, then you can do the same with internal or personal beliefs. To do so, you need to learn to *doubt*.

See if you can become a skeptic about your own beliefs. By now I hope you realize that any belief you have that keeps you from your goal of "happy survival" may well be nonsensical and irrational.

Why hold onto old beliefs that hurt you instead of help you? Begin by trying to stand as a doubter on your own behalf.

The people of San Francisco generally felt secure as they readied themselves to view the third game of the 1989 World Series. They assumed the stadium would hold and the earth would remain stationary. After the quake, for days and weeks, they became doubters. They no longer felt secure with their feet on the hard ground. That ground could move because it did move once already.

The same attitude needs to be true for you. Those sacred beliefs that get you into trouble are not built on firm ground. Doubt their accuracy, just as San Franciscans doubted their own safety after the quake. Your beliefs about yourself will change only when you throw a good dose of doubt into the mix. Please do yourself a favor now and work on doubting those old automatic beliefs that hurt you personally and cause you stress and discomfort.

Principle 5

Keep an open mind to all information coming your way.

You've heard it. Maybe even said it yourself: "Don't confuse me with the facts. My mind's made up." I have a friend who says (and believes), "I may not always be right, but I am never in doubt." Most of us, I'm afraid, think we're pretty open to new ideas and input. I'm offended if someone thinks I'm close-minded. I imagine you are, too. We think of ourselves as open, intellectually honest and curious about life. The one thing we are not is narrow-minded.

I hope that's true. But the very resistance you show to the thought of being close-minded may prove the point. If an open-minded person were accused of having a closed mind, I imagine he or she would entertain the possibility of it being so. Unfortunately, when it comes to your deep, automatic and personal beliefs, most likely you are somewhat closed-minded. At this level it may seem difficult for you to accept new information, even if that information challenges your old beliefs.

When it comes to your most personal beliefs, you tend to resist change. Your beliefs have been your companions for years. You won't cut them loose with the first breeze of a new thought. You hold on, loyally defending your automatic thoughts, whether or not they are accurate reflections of reality.

Roger von Oech wrote a book on creativity called *A Kick in the Seat of the Pants* (Harper & Row, 1986). In it he points out how hard it is to see a new point of view once you have locked in on your original view. At one point he writes, "If Jack's in love, he's no judge of Jill's beauty." And also, "It is difficult to see the picture when you are inside the frame."

Your challenge is to get outside your own frame – to see in a new way, to *want* to take in new information. If you have beliefs that create dissatisfying feelings and behaviors that you want to change, you need to open yourself to brand new viewpoints. The renowned psychologist Abraham Maslow once said, "People who are only good with hammers see every problem as a nail."

Basically you have two mental functions: one is to *perceive* and the other is to *judge*. One of these functions tends to be more dominant for you. If you are primarily a "perceiver," it will be a little easier for you to remain open to new information. If you are more the "judger," then you tend to cut off information in order to get to the action. You are more of a doer.

If you hear yourself jumping to conclusions quickly about other people's behavior, you block further perceptions. Your mind works fast. You want to "cut to the chase." You probably don't shop around for the best bargain. You go to one store, get a price and buy the item.

One of the better examples of the perceiving/judging power comes from the Bible. The Pharisees brought a woman to Jesus. They claimed she had been caught in the act of adultery. They asked Jesus to judge her. He *looked* at her, according to the story. In other words, he simply perceived her. He then said those famous words, "Whoever is without sin, let him cast the first stone." He didn't judge her. He only perceived her. He did give her a friendly piece of advice, though, suggesting that she not get into the adultery thing anymore.

When it comes to your basic beliefs, I want to encourage you strongly to fight for an open mind. Allow yourself to take in as much information as possible. Realize how judgmental you may be about yourself based on your beliefs from long ago. If you believe negatively about yourself, then understand that you allow in only beliefs that are negative. Because you have put on very dark glasses and see only the shadows, you have to begin believing there are other, more positive views out there. I realize this demands an act of faith. If you haven't seen the sun, it's hard to believe it exists. But believe it. Work to take off the dark glasses and look for the sunlight. It's there waiting for you to discover it.

At first when you take in new information, it will feel strange and uncomfortable. You will say, "I can see it with my mind, but it doesn't *feel* right." Remember what it was like when you first learned to ride a two-wheeled bike. You felt clumsy and awkward. You fell frequently. You wondered if you'd ever get it. Yet once you got it, it never left you. It felt right. It fit. The same is true of your beliefs. At first new beliefs feel strange. They don't fit well. But gradually you "get it." Once you do, your new beliefs become as automatic as your old ones.

Starting out with *doubt* about your old, automatic beliefs and being *open* to all new information places you in the best position for change. Doubt and openness prime you to become aware; they challenge the beliefs that negatively influence your feelings and behaviors. With these two stances you ready yourself for the challenge of new freedom – the freedom from old feelings and behaviors that have led to conflict, upset, worry and sadness.

Principle 6

Actively challenge old beliefs that cause unwanted feelings and behaviors.

For this one, get out the fighter in you. To change your unwanted feelings and behaviors, you need all your energy to fight the old beliefs that sit stoically in your pre-conscious mind. Remember the ABCs of rational thinking that we discussed on page 17 of this book?

A. An *activating event* takes place.

B. Your old, automatic *beliefs* kick in.

C. You respond with feeling and behavioral *consequences*.

You understand that process. Now comes the next step, "D." You *dispute* "B," your old automatic *beliefs*. Then you challenge very actively and aggressively the beliefs that cause "C," the feeling and behavioral consequences you don't like.

Try disputing your beliefs in several ways:

Verbally

Talk to yourself. Think up arguments to use against your beliefs. Repeat the new thoughts frequently. You might even write them down, just to see them out in front of you. Furthermore, it's very helpful to speak your new disputing thoughts out loud. You can do that with another person or alone. I think one of the best places to "do" psychology is in the car when you're driving alone. Talk out loud to yourself. Let yourself hear with your outer ears what you're trying to say inside. When you do this, you might want to keep your car windows closed. If you don't, other folks at the stop light might wonder about you and call the police or the dog catcher.

Talking out your old and new beliefs with another person can be very helpful as well. That person can help you more clearly identify the sabotaging beliefs that you might be missing. He or she can also help you think of new, challenging thoughts to replace the old ones. The other person can push you, challenge you and cajole you. He or she can help you see from a different point of view and can help you climb out of your old picture frame.

With Passion

When you challenge old beliefs, you need to exert lots of energy. This is hard work. I want to encourage you to get enthused, get angry with those old beliefs. They have negatively affected your life for a long time. You no longer need to be enslaved by those burdensome bullies.

Think your new and challenging thoughts, but do so with emotion. Say, "Darn it anyway. It's stupid to go on believing anybody even cares if I get up in the group and ask a question." Say it with feeling. Say it like you believe it. At the beginning you may have to play act a little. You won't feel convinced. But at least you can *sound* convinced. Pretending is a valuable tool in coming to believe. Actors and actresses play roles. At a certain point they actually believe they are the characters they're portraying. With your beliefs the same can occur. If you get into your new beliefs and continue dressing yourself in them and reciting them with enthusiasm, you're more likely to get comfortable with them and come to really believe them.

With Action

One of the best ways of challenging your old thoughts is by *acting* against them. Generally, beliefs don't change if you sit in a chair and meditate, although that would probably help. You want to begin acting in ways that reflect your new thinking even if it doesn't "feel" right. In graduate school I used to be shy about telling people what I needed from them. I could be in a restaurant, get a cold hamburger, have the waitress ask how my meal was and I could still say "fine." It wasn't fine, but I didn't want to cause problems. My "enemy belief" was, "If I hassle her, she won't like me."

Some of my colleagues – graduate students in psychology – decided to help me out. They took me to a little off-campus diner. Without my knowledge, they took the salt and pepper shakers off the table. They also removed the ketchup and mustard. When I ordered my food, I needed those condiments. They insisted that I ask for them. I would have just eaten my burger without ketchup because I didn't want to bother the waitress. But my colleagues forced me to pay attention to my needs and ask that those needs be satisfied. I resisted. They insisted. Since I was outnumbered, I capitulated. Thus began my active, behavioral attack on my "enemy belief" that waitresses wouldn't like me if I made my needs known to them.

Years have gone by. I now have a different belief about diners and waitresses, which goes like this: "Waitresses want to please me and will generally go out of their way to accommodate me." I changed my belief because first I was forced by others to do so, and then I forced myself to act against my old belief and in support of my new belief. I began to get new evidence that asking for a hamburger to be reheated was not a crime. In fact, most waitresses acted as if it were *their* fault the burger was cold. They would apologize several times and often bring a new one. Sometimes they even threw in a free dessert, although that doesn't happen much anymore.

Acting against your old beliefs gets you emotionally involved in your own change. While your head has to do the changing and challenging of your beliefs, your action against those beliefs gets your whole self into the game. Acting also gives you dramatic new information that adds weight to your mind's fight against the "enemy beliefs." So act against your sabotaging beliefs, while challenging them verbally and arguing against them with passion.

Lisa and Tony had gone together for two years. Their relationship had been filled with passion and delight, arguments and disappointments. Tony finally decided to end the relationship. He told Lisa. It "broke her heart." She went into a depression that got worse and worse. Finally she sought professional help.

What did we have here?

A. Tony's breaking off the relationship served as the *activating event.*

C. Lisa reacted with depression and withdrawal from life. (The "C" step feels as if it comes before the "B" step. Lisa experienced the activating event and quickly felt the *consequences.* Then she could go back and look for her beliefs and thoughts.)

B. With the help of a counselor, Lisa began to look at her *beliefs* about breaking up with Tony. She discovered her beliefs:

   • I'll never see him again. I can't live without him.
   • My life is ruined forever.
   • I'll never get over this. I will feel empty all my life.
   • I'll never find another person to love. I'll grow old alone.
   • I am not a lovable person. Something must be wrong with me. No man will ever want me.

Those beliefs caused Lisa long-term depression. To suffer loss in the present is one thing. But Lisa carried her significant loss into eternity. Notice all the "nevers" in her thinking. Also notice that her orientation was toward the future, a sure bet to cause internal suffering.

Eventually Lisa began disputing and challenging her enemy beliefs. She tried to think differently, even though her effort was half-hearted at first. She thought, "Wait. I *am* lovable. Tony loved me. He must have seen something good in me. He didn't stop loving me because I was a bad person. He stopped because we argued so much." She also tried to believe, "The present moment is all I have. I want to give myself over to it as best I can." And she added another new thought: "People get over these kinds of things.

In fact, most happily married people have probably experienced a break-up in some relationship along the way. People do recover, and I will too. I want to get back into life now."

Armed with these tentative beliefs, Lisa then worked to "mean them when I say them." She got angry with Tony. She said to herself, "He made a poor judgment in dumping me. He doesn't know what he lost." She insisted with herself every morning to get right up and face the day. Enter it, she would, and live only the moment. "Darn it, all I have is this moment. I'm going to give it all the gusto I have."

Finally she forced herself to *act* that way. She went back to her regular routine. She pushed herself to begin talking with people again, laughing again and planning social events for the weekends with her friends.

Gradually, through the hard work of disputing, challenging and acting against her sabotaging beliefs about the future and about her break-up with Tony, Lisa began to let go of the depression. With time, but mostly with her own hard work, she returned to the state of animation and enthusiasm for life that she had known before the problems with Tony. And yes, the story has a happy ending. She did find another man, Jeffrey, whom she married. I hope they are living "happily ever after."

Principle 7

**Dramatic and demanding thoughts need
to be challenged in special ways.**

"I'll never again find a woman to love." "I'll always be trapped in this dead-end job." "I'm sure my headache is an inoperable brain tumor." This kind of dramatic, jump-to-incredible-conclusions thinking creates high levels of anxiety and worry. It invades peace of mind and hangs like black clouds over the most enjoyable occasions.

"He shouldn't have spoken to me like that." "I should have gotten a raise." "She must be on time." "He has to clean his room before he goes out to play." These demanding, insistent thoughts result in frustration, anger and upset. They strip away contentment and erode the gentle flow of patience and tolerance.

Dramatic thinking leads to anxiety and fear. Demanding thinking causes anger and resentment. Both these thinking patterns are more fully explored in the **Life Skills Series** books *Overcoming Fear* and *Reducing Anger*. I want to touch on them here, however, because they're so central to the skill of thinking reasonably. Of all the irrational beliefs I have heard, dramatic and demanding thoughts are among the most common. From childhood on you have heard the dramatic and the demanding. "If you keep making those faces, one day your face will stay that way." "You should eat your food because kids are starving in China." "If you think impure thoughts you will burn in hell forever." "You'll also burn in hell if you don't obey your parents." "God is a vengeful, judging God."

Challenging dramatic thoughts and replacing them with more realistic considerations brings about calm and peace. Worry and fear stick to your visceral walls like bad cholesterol does to your arteries. You can lower cholesterol by eliminating fats from your diet. You can reduce worry by dieting from dramatic and catastrophic thinking.

Worry and fear occur because you think into the *future*. You anticipate the worst possible outcome. A couple I know, Sue and Joe, occasionally give talks together on marriage. Sue gets nervous. She beings worrying about a week before. Some of those talks take place on the weekend and in conjunction with a meal. If the event is scheduled for Saturday night, by Saturday morning she has reached high anxiety. By the time of the talk she is saying to her husband, "Joe, I don't want to do any more talks. This is the last one." Then she gives the presentation with her husband. The audience responds to her very positively. On the way out of the building, she says to him, "You know, I probably could give these talks with you again."

The anxiety is gone, replaced by relief and peace. All Sue's worry was for naught. In fact, afterward she is willing to give another talk. What happened? She changed her thinking. Beforehand she thought, "These people expect me to be an entertainer. I'm not that. I'm an educator. But if I don't make them laugh and they don't have a great old time, they will not like me. I will fail. And that will be awful."

Part of Sue's thinking was accurate. She isn't an entertainer or a comedian. She's an educator. But she was inaccurate about people expecting to be entertained. She concluded incorrectly and dramatically that they would not like her if she wasn't funny and clever. And she missed reality completely by thinking she would fail if they didn't laugh. Even if she did "fail" somehow, it would be uncomfortable but certainly not "awful."

After the talk, she realized once again that she wasn't an entertainer. But she also learned that the women, in particular, fully appreciated her warmth and honesty about the woman's point of view in marriage. She realized they weren't even looking for a comedian to serve as dessert to their meal. They wanted exactly what she gave them—a woman's point of view about men and relationships. That, she figured, she could offer. So with her changed thinking about giving talks, she came to a new conclusion – she could continue giving talks with her husband – sometimes. The next time Joe schedules such a talk for both of them, perhaps Sue will remember her new viewpoint and think positive thoughts beforehand. That way she will be able to enjoy her entire Saturday as well as the banquet meal right before the talk.

Anger works a little differently. It arises out of demanding thoughts that insist something should be a certain way. If it doesn't work out that way and you keep insisting it must, you become angry.

The neighbor's cat kept coming into Ralph's yard. He got angry every time he saw that cat prancing around his bushes and trees. He thought, "Cats shouldn't be allowed outside without a leash. Anyway, my neighbor ought to watch where his cat is going. He should keep her in his yard." Those few thoughts were enough to trigger anger whenever the cat appeared in Ralph's yard.

Ralph chose not to talk with his neighbor about controlling the cat. He thought, "Talking to him could start World War III. I can't stand having anyone upset with me." (The drama in these thoughts created some fear in Ralph, stopping him from talking with his neighbor in a kindly way about his concerns.) Anyway, since Ralph decided not to take any action regarding the cat, he had to either live with his anger every time the cat arrived or change his point of view to become more accepting of the cat's presence, thus reducing his anger.

To become more accepting, Ralph needed to challenge his basic beliefs about cats in his yard and his neighbor's responsibilities. What might have been some challenging new thoughts he could have used to replace the old angry thoughts? How about:

- Generally, you don't see cats on leashes. I can't expect that here.
- The cat isn't harming anything in my yard. She doesn't even poop in my bushes.
- The cat may actually be keeping the rabbits out of my yard and doing me a service.
- Although I *wish* Bob (the neighbor) would watch his cat, he doesn't. My insistence doesn't change the reality. So I need to simply accept it.
- In the great scheme of life's events, having a cat romp through my yard occasionally is a very small issue.

By trying to insert these challenging and new thoughts into his mental process, Ralph worked at letting go of his anger. He made the cat a less powerful issue by trying to view the cat's presence as positive, or at least as not such a big deal. Gradually he learned to accept the cat's presence without any anger. Oh yes, one other new thought was helpful to him: "If Bob keeps letting his cat run around, there is a good chance she will run into the road and get hit by a truck."

Identify, then, as best as you can any thoughts you have that cause worry or anger. They will usually be dramatic and demanding. Isolate those thoughts and then get out your challenging skills. Insert new, more realistic and less catastrophic thoughts to reduce worry and fear. Create more positive and accepting thoughts to fight against anger.

Principle 8

Along with challenging and changing your thoughts, you can learn to view your environment selectively.

Viewing your environment selectively means paying attention only to those aspects of your world under your control at the moment. The most dramatic example of viewing your environment selectively comes from Beirut, Lebanon. In *From Bierut to Jerusalem* (Doubleday, 1989), a book about the wars, strife, terrorism and killings that have gone on in the Middle East over the past 75 years. Thomas L. Friedman explains the coping mechanisms of the Beirutis. Those who best survived mentally during the Israeli invasion in 1982 did so by closing their eyes to the bombing, bloodshed and death around them. Instead they focused on their present immediate situation and on those things under their own control.

If a citizen was driving down the street and a car bomb went off two blocks ahead of him, he simply backed up and took another street to his destination. If fighting was taking place 50 miles away, a father would go on with life as usual, not worrying about the shooting. If fighting broke out in the street next to his, he would pay no attention. Only if the fighting occurred outside his doorway would he be concerned and take action to protect his family.

I sincerely hope that you and I never need to exert this amount of selective attention. But the dramatic point applies well to dealing with runaway thoughts that cause you to suffer. You do your best to block out what is not under your control and focus on those aspects of your environment that you do control. If you're on your way to play tennis and all the while are worrying about a forecast of rain, you cannot enjoy a friendly match. You can't control the weather, but you can take charge of getting yourself to the tennis court. Focus on that.

You can't control whether your supervisors will enjoy your presentation, but you can work to do your best no matter how they respond. You can't stop a tall man from sitting in front of you at the movie, but you can concentrate on the movie even if you have to strain your neck a little. You can't always get your kids to act like adults, but you can appreciate how inventive and creative they are in getting out of work around the house.

By focusing on what you control, you become active in your life. You make things happen. When you pay attention to what you have no control over, you become passive and still. Into the vacuum of your inactivity rushes even more suffering thoughts, leading you to further lethargy. On and on the vicious cycle goes. You break that bitter wheel by seeing what you *can* do and then doing it. The more actively involved you become, the less you will attend to the awful realities over which you have no control.

Chapter Three

Beliefs that Lead to Peace of Mind

I've talked with you about changing your thought patterns when those thoughts cause feelings and behaviors you don't like and you want to change. But you can also work on your thoughts when no particular problem is present. In fact, this might be the best time to make some mental changes.

Over the years I have recognized in myself and others certain types of thoughts that create a general view of life that doesn't work well. These thought patterns routinely cause you to suffer. You notice that when you're not suffering and when you're free from distress, you are hearing more constructive and helpful thoughts arising from within you.

Let's take a look at the most prominent suffering and non-suffering thoughts. Once you recognize what they are, you can begin the disciplined work of changing your patterns into peace-making thoughts and views.

Descriptive Rather Than Judgmental

"Nobody made you the judge," I keep telling clients who assign the label of right and wrong to every act. While judgments are certainly necessary to your daily existence, many judgments – especially negative ones – create a suffering mind.

Try something the next time you walk through a shopping mall. Attempt to *describe* to yourself what you see without passing any judgments. You might see a hairdo that has every spike, curl, chop and color imaginable. Simply describe it to yourself: "I see a girl's hair that has been tinted orange, spiked at the forehead, shaved on the right side and flowing to her shoulder on the left." Try not making any judgment about the hair. Don't let yourself say, "How dumb! Young people are so weird. I would never let my daughter out in public looking like that."

Notice as you walk through the mall how easy it is to pass judgment on almost anything in sight. You can hold court regarding the structure and layout of the mall, the lighting, the prices of items, the type of merchandise and the number and location of rest rooms. ("Why do they always hide them behind the pots and pans department where nobody would ever look? They should put them out in the open." Oops, that's a judgment. See how easy it is.)

As you have seen throughout this book, *negative* judgments are the villains that get you into trouble and cause your suffering.

Years ago, the comedian George Carlin identified seven dirty words that could not be said on television. He then proceeded to go around the country announcing these words at his live shows. Times have changed and several of those words can now be spoken on television. In our psychological world I believe there are also certain dirty words – 14 of them. They sound tamer than Carlin's seven, but I think they are much more destructive. Here they are:

Good - Bad
Right - Wrong
Appropriate - Inappropriate
Proper - Improper
Fair - Unfair
Should - Ought - Must - Have To

These 14 words get you into emotional trouble with yourself. Applied to yourself, they readily cause guilt, shame and a sense of inadequacy. "Did I do it *right?*" "That was quite *inappropriate* of me." "I *shouldn't* have acted that way." "That was a *bad* way to feel." Oftentimes, you draw a conclusion following these kinds of statements, a conclusion that smacks you right in the ego. "I *shouldn't* have acted that way. What a jerk I am. I am so clumsy when it comes to relating to other people. I *ought* to just hole up and die."

When these 14 words get applied to others, you tend to become angry with them, or put them down, or both. "He *shouldn't* have spoken to me like that. I have no respect for a man who acts that way." Such a judgment generates anger and a break in the relationship. "What an *unfair* grade. The teacher doesn't like me. She's a nerd anyway." "She *ought* to be more patient with her kids. They're going to grow up with a complex if she's not careful." "He's such a *bad* little boy. He never listens." These judgmental conclusions serve no worthwhile purpose and only cause you irritation.

I realize that from a moral point of view we need terms like right and wrong, good and bad. But they are not particularly useful from a psychological point of view. Instead of using these words, I suggest that you think in terms of inserting the following:

Useful - Not useful
Helpful - Unhelpful

These five expressions work much better in assessing the effects of your own or others' behavior or feelings. The only slight judgment here focuses on what works and doesn't work rather than on the *value* of the response. "Helpful/unhelpful," in fact, is simply descriptive of an event's impact. These words allow you to change your response without beating up on yourself or someone else.

By thinking in terms of describing events rather than judging them, you create a mindset that allows for considerable flexibility. Remember, nobody appointed you judge – certainly not of other people's lives. And, I would suggest, not even of your own. Instead of judging, describe your behavior to yourself and decide only if it was helpful or not helpful to you and to others. If it was not helpful, then you can peacefully go about changing the behavior without putting on the sackcloth and ashes.

Unique Thoughts Rather Than Comparative

"I'm a better tennis player than you are." "You're a better money manager than I am." (I wish *that* were reversed.) "You're cuter than I am." "I probably have a higher IQ than Jim." "My kids made the A Honor Roll and Sandy's didn't." "Why can't you be like your sister?"

These and a wide variety of other comparative thoughts cause suffering. You and I live in a one-up/one-down society. We go from the bottom of the ladder to the top, back to the bottom. The yo-yo effect may level out some in adulthood. When you're one-up, you feel only superficially good, because under the delight lies the realization that you can be outdone by another soon. Business people know that. When their widget is selling well, another widget, bigger and better, is in production and will hit the market in six months. A shopping mall near my home was built 10 years ago to much fanfare. It did great business. But two years ago, a new mall with better and brighter stores was built three blocks away. Already the old mall is losing customers and slowly dying. When you fall to one-down, you suffer.

More helpful to you are non-comparative or unique thoughts. You give power to what you focus on. If you attend to how others are doing, where they go on vacation, how much money, status or power they have in relation to you, eventually you suffer. Focus instead on yourself, on what you have, on your satisfactions, on your position and so on. Tell yourself you have only you and your loved ones to attend to. You were not created to measure up to someone else's standards. Life isn't a contest that pits you against your neighbor or sibling to see who gets farthest in the race toward success.

Unique or individualistic thinking keeps you in your own psychological backyard. It also allows you to enjoy and celebrate other people's successes. If you find yourself begrudging others' achievements or good fortune, then you know you're a highly comparative thinker. Why cause yourself to suffer unduly? Let go of focusing on others' positions. Value where you are in life's journey. Celebrate your present spot in this world because it's your *only* spot. It's yours and no one else's. You're there, so enter it, embrace it and live it to its fullest. (More on this skill in the **Life Skills Series** book, *Meeting Life Head On*.)

Cooperative Rather Than Competitive

Closely aligned to comparative thoughts are competitive thoughts. One flows out of the other. You know you're in competition when you hear yourself keeping score. Husbands and wives do this: "I went two times to your mother's, and you went to only one movie with me." "You spend at least twice as much time with your friends as you do with me." Friends and acquaintances do the same: "I called him three times, and he has not called me once." "We *always* do what she wants to do and *never* what I want to do." The score in this case is one million to nothing. Now, that's a wipe-out.

Kids get into competitive thinking with each other. One doesn't want a scoop of ice cream smaller than the other. Certainly one kid can't do more housework than the other. Outside the home you hear,

"My dad can beat up your dad" or the infamous Smothers Brothers line, "Mom loves you more than she loves me."

In competitive thinking you tend to remain focused on yourself – on what you want rather than on what the other needs. The point of reference is you instead of him or her. You think in terms of how very much *you* have given and how very little *you* have gotten in return. If, in fact, you felt you received a lot from the other, you would rarely consider how much you had given.

Cooperative thinking, on the other hand, moves toward lending the helping hand and not *counting* (there's that word again) the cost. If you concentrate on the other person's needs and desires without measuring them against your own, you can create a more cooperative mindset. Naturally, this works better if the other person has the same cooperative mindset and is responding to your needs and desires.

When you think cooperatively, you focus on how both of you can win. You figure out what adjustments each of you must make in order for you each to gain your goals. The other person's gain is then not seen as your loss. Together you seek the best for both of you. Successful married couples, for example, concentrate on pleasing each other. They focus their attention on what the other needs rather than on what they, themselves, are not getting. If both parties try meeting the other's needs, they rarely pay attention to themselves. By taking care of the other, they find the other taking care of them. It takes two to create a cooperative relationship.

Informative Rather Than Interpretive

Information comes from outside of you. It must be dug out, pursued and integrated. It takes hard work to sort through it all and put it in order. Interpretation, on the other hand, is the lazy person's way of learning. Searching for more information, creating a detailed and complete mental picture, takes much more energy than having a sketchy outline and filling in the gaping holes with your easily-arrived-at interpretations. Interpretation comes from inside of you. It grabs onto old information and brings it to the present issue. It takes little work and disregards accuracy. It assumes that it always fills in correctly and fully. Interpretations are your subjective efforts to fill in the missing blanks left by a lack of information. These interpretations skew the facts according to your prejudices.

For example, on a day when you feel blue, your interpretation of a rainy morning might include statements such as, "The sun has not shone for weeks. The weather in this state is awful. I wish I could move, but I'm trapped here. I'll never get out of my present job and lifestyle." On another rainy day when you feel peppy and energetic, you might interpret, "What a great day to get all my desk work done. I'll do that, then make a fire, curl up and read that book. I could use more days like this."

Seeking more and more information reduces the amount of interpreting and filling in the blanks that you do. The more information you have, the less interpreting you do. The less information you have, the more interpreting you do. (For more on this read the **Life Skills Series** book, *Communicating*.)

Optimistic Rather Than Pessimistic

Do you see the half empty or half full glass? Do you notice the donut or the hole? Do you expect the worst so you won't be too disappointed if the best doesn't happen? "Two men looked out from prison bars. One saw mud, the other stars." You have heard all these turns of phrase. Actually these old sayings apply well to this issue of taking a positive or negative viewpoint of life's events.

Here especially you give power to what you focus on. You have a choice about what you attend to. You can focus on how much you don't know about fixing the dripping faucet, or you can attend to all the ways you might be able to go about getting it fixed. Either you can see yourself as an inadequate homeowner, or you can consider yourself very resourceful in finding ways and means of getting the job done.

Obviously, negative thinking leads to depression. In a piece of research I read a while ago psychologists concluded that people who viewed the world negatively became depressed more easily than others. Those who viewed the world realistically also tended toward depression. In many ways, I suppose, the real world is in a fairly depressive state. So it's understandable that those who viewed the world through positive glasses lived depression-free and much happier than the other two groups. Those who viewed the world positively may have been a little out of touch with reality, but they lived more joyful and contented lives. Perhaps the message here is to slightly distort your world view in a positive direction because it works.

By reporting this research to you, I'm not suggesting that you deny reality. No. I believe some realities out there are difficult and quite awful. I think, though, that you can look at those negatives, acknowledge their presence and even respond to them as you are able. But you don't need to *dwell* on those negatives. You can say yes to them and then direct your attention to more positive, life-giving realities.

Years ago I directed a Justice and Peace Center involved in social concerns issues. We constantly saw the dark side of politics and life. It was, in fact, quite depressing and pessimistic. After work I had to consciously shut off the heavy stuff we were dealing with. Friends of mine would invite me to attend "socially relevant movies." I refused to go. I wanted only to be entertained. I wanted to laugh and watch silly, slapstick humor. I had made a choice to not focus on the negatives, even though I acknowledged their presence.

Again, you give power to what you focus on. Attend to the negative and you grow pessimistic and depressed. Focus on the positive, and you feel more optimistic and energized to live your life fully.

Constructive Rather Than Destructive

Most likely if you think positively, you will also think constructively. I'm sure you have been in brainstorming meetings, throwing creative ideas around the room. Inevitably one or a few people have poured cold water on any new idea that surfaced. "Oh, that won't work, because . . . " "It would cost way too much." "We don't have the people to do the job." Such destructive thinking never lets creative genius get off the ground. On the other hand, supporting ideas, adding to them, fleshing them out adds a great spark to your life and to others'.

You can tear down, or you can build up. It's your choice. You can look at a reality and see the possibilities for growth and development. Or you can notice the limitations and the potential failures. There is a saying floating around parenting seminars that expresses the same thing: "Your children become the products of your hopes or your fears." If you keep seeing what can go wrong, it will. But if you keep hoping for and anticipating what can come true, it more likely will do so.

Thinking constructively leads you to recognize more options in your own life. It further allows you to become encouraging to others rather than critical. You see the good and wonderful potential in each person or issue rather than the negative, and limitations of each reality. What a much nicer way to live!

Flexible Rather Than Demanding

Please work on this one. Over the years I have become convinced that flexibility, perhaps more than anything else, leads to peace of mind and to satisfying, conflict-free relationships. Flexible thinking means going with the flow. If you don't judge and don't do a lot of interpreting, then flexibility shouldn't be too difficult.

Demanding, rigid thinking creates great stress internally and in your relationships. If you are cursed with rigid thinking, then you find yourself spending a lot of time forcing the proverbial round peg into the square hole. You know what kind of tension this creates. You roam the world attempting to get everything to *fit* into your constructs of how it's all supposed to work. "The sun should shine on my vacation days." "My kids should take personal responsibility for doing their homework." "People should drive cars the way I do." "My spouse should always be on time." On it goes.

Unfortunately, although you can go around making up all the rules and regulations you want about how the world should operate, you have very little power to enforce your rules. The result for you? Increased frustration and stress, leading to anger, rage, ulcers, conflict, broken relationships and general unhappiness. Why keep insisting that the world operate according to your map? Especially when such insistence ends up in rage and ulcers?

Flexibility, on the other hand, feels tolerant and accepting. It allows you to recognize that other people have different points of view. They learned to drive, cook, dress, talk and work from unique sets of circumstances. Who is to say one is *right* and the other *wrong?* (Two dirty words there.) People are the way they are. Period. You may not *like* how they act, but can you accept it, live with it? Maybe in the future you can even appreciate their unique way of doing something.

Flexibility begins with you. Can you accept yourself with your little foibles and limitations? Or do you demand perfection in all you do? Do you fight against and deny your own weaknesses? Or are you able to appreciate them and even laugh at them at times? Flexible thinking demands a great deal of self-acceptance. Once that's in place, you won't have much trouble accepting others' imperfections and the many limitations of our world.

Broad Rather Than Narrow

Wise people see the world through wide-angle lenses. Have you ever noticed a grandfather or an older aunt who takes life in stride? They tend not to sweat the details. They don't worry about things as they used to. They see the bigger picture. In the sweeping scope of their own personal histories, the issues now brought to them get placed in a much larger perspective.

Young people don't have such wide-angle views. They see things up close and much more narrowly. Consequently, they make issues much bigger than they actually are. They then respond in much more powerful and dramatic ways.

If you place a tea cup three inches from your nose, it looks very large. It dominates your visual screen. It takes up all your eye's energy. But if you step back from the tea cup 20 feet, you see it sitting amid 50 other dishes, utensils and linens, making a fine Thanksgiving setting. The tea cup looks different in this setting, much smaller and less dominant. You see the tea cup from the wider perspective of the entire table.

When it comes to personal problems, you tend to put the issue three inches from your nose. Then it becomes gigantic in its proportions. It occupies your entire mind and attention. You can think of nothing else. It would be more helpful for you to step back and attempt to see the issue from a distance. It will look different, most likely less traumatic and catastrophic.

Bringing issues too close to your nose leads to over-dramatizing them. You place way too much power in those events. The result is often considerable upset, worry, anger, sadness and guilt. Gaining the broad view helps reduce the intensity of an issue. The child's misbehavior, the lost sale, the IRS audit all appear less powerful in the wide view of your life.

Unfortunately, this wide-angle view usually comes only with age and experience. The longer you live, the easier it is to get the big picture. If you're a young person, you need time to stretch your view to fill the wide screen. Due to a lack of experience, you need to stand back and pause in your busy life in order to frame the issues in a bigger way. Experience and reflective time, then, are the avenues leading to the big picture – and with it, wisdom.

Light Rather Than Serious

When still a pre-schooler, my daughter, Amy, was a great pouter. She could stick that lower lip out further than anyone I knew. It used to annoy me. I'd get irritated with her. My irritation, though, didn't stop her pouts.

One day by accident I pouted back when she pouted. I then said, "I wonder if I can pout better than you." We had a little pouting contest. She won, hands down. I declared her the winner. We both laughed. She quit pouting.

From then on every time Amy pouted, I'd pout back. She would then pout even more. We'd laugh and the pout was gone. She's growing up, and I just realized that she never pouts any more. She outgrew it. And here I must have been worried that she would pout all her life whenever she didn't get her way. I guess I worried about nothing.

Anyway, I learned something very important about myself when Amy was a young pouter. I realized that a little humor helps keep me from making issues bigger than they need to be. Had I taken Amy's pouting seriously, we would have engaged in great battles. Lightening up broke the tension between us and kept me free from ulcers.

Perhaps you have noticed becoming more serious as you've grown older. I think this is a natural tendency as responsibilities are added to your life. Remember high school and college? You were carefree. You could be a "wild and crazy guy." Now, you are "grown up" and have a job, a car, perhaps a family. Bills need to be paid, the house painted and the garbage taken to the curb. Life has become filled with tasks that need to get done. A friend told me of her neighbor who plays in a band. His business card reads, "We've got jobs, we've got kids, we've got mortgages ... we *need* rock and roll."

Try putting the fun back in, okay? Learn again to enjoy your friends, your spouse, your kids. Do something a little wild once in a while. Don't take everything so seriously. Relax, take it easy and get into the delights of life. The child in you still lives! She wants to come out and play. The adult part of you knows that's not possible all the time. But you could give her some freedom. You could allow her opportunities to run in the fields, look for frogs, ride her bike to McDonalds or stay up late and watch an old-time movie, eating popcorn and drinking Kool-Aid. Life seems so short. To spend all of your time carrying out your serious responsibilities makes it appear even shorter. Balance is the key word here – balance between the responsible adult in you and the carefree, fun-loving child.

Present Rather Than Future or Past

Thinking in the present helps you remain free from suffering. While you may experience pain in the present moment, most of your suffering occurs in the past or the future. Worry, for example, always happens when you focus on the future: "I wonder if he will pick me up when he said." "Will my kids get into drugs?" "I hope I don't make a fool of myself at the board meeting." At the present time all may be well in your world. But by focusing on the future, you bring worry into your present.

The same is true of the past. By thinking backwards, especially about dark events, you relive the suffering you once endured. The anger you had over being fired comes back today with much of its original power. The pain of a rejection can still be felt years later. The loss of a parent through death is recalled with sorrow at Christmas time.

Again, this mental principle comes into play: You give power to what you focus on. By flipping back to the past, especially the hurtful past, you give it power again. By attending to possible future tragedies, you give events that haven't even happened yet power as well. Thinking in the present moment allows you to live quite free from suffering, even though you experience moments of pain.

This doesn't mean you should never think in the past or future.

Many of your happiest thoughts come from your remembrances of past occasions. Also, anticipating happy events, such as vacations and holidays, can bring much delight. Basically, I'm suggesting you avoid past and future thoughts that lead to worry, guilt, sadness or anger. Those that lead to joy and peace can be entertained as frequently as you like. Generally, present thinking serves you more effectively than past or future thinking.

So there you are. If you can learn to let go of your suffering thoughts and insert more peaceful, calming thoughts, you will come a long way in feeling good about yourself and life around you. Certainly there are strains and tribulations in life. They cause pain, and you won't always be able to control them. But you can take charge of how much you suffer around that pain. You do it by taking control of your thoughts.

Principle 9

**Be patient and work hard to change
old beliefs into new beliefs.**

Old beliefs don't die easily. You have been practicing some of these beliefs for 20, 30 or 40 years. They don't simply go away when you challenge them once or twice. So be prepared to do battle. Stay with the project. It will pay off for you.

But let me explain how this change takes place. First, you have your old beliefs. These create your feelings and behaviors, the ones you want to change. By inserting new beliefs, you begin to challenge and break down the old beliefs. However, the old beliefs don't simply vanish. They remain, still generating the old feelings. So for a while you might become discouraged. You have been working on new beliefs, but you still have the old feelings (because you still also have the old thoughts). For a while it feels like this plan of action isn't working. You're trying to think new, more reasonable thoughts but are still coming up with lousy feelings. Hang in there!

Gradually you begin breaking down those old thought patterns. The new thoughts begin winning the battle for prominence in your mind. As that occurs, your old feelings weaken and new, more satisfying feelings are created by your new belief patterns. If I graphed it for you it would look like this:

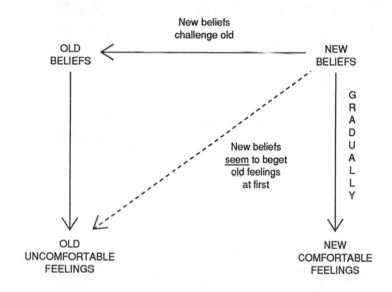

Next week you realize you have a dentist's appointment. You immediately get nervous, hands sweating, fear mounting. You don't like having that anxious feeling all week. You decide to challenge the old thoughts that kick in your fear. So you start inserting new, more reasonable thoughts. But you still feel anxious. At this point you need to stay with the fight. Continue challenging, even though your old feelings still dominate your emotional menu.

Gradually, as the week goes on, your new thoughts begin taking hold. As they do, your old beliefs, many of them originating from childhood, begin to diminish in power. As they do, your anxiety begins to leave. By Dentist Day you may still feel some light anxiety, but I hope you feel more calm than you have in the past. I won't guarantee that the day will come where you have so changed your thinking that you will jump for joy at the opportunity to go to the dentist. But you can, with work, significantly reduce your fear.

So be patient. Allow your new thoughts time to take hold. Realize that until then, those old uncomfortable feelings will hang around. Old thought patterns don't die easily.

Chapter Four

Developing this Skill with Others

R emember that at the beginning of this book I mentioned how we all believe our thinking is accurate and logical? I hope by now you're willing to doubt a little. Working on this skill of thinking reasonably either with another person or with a group can help you cast more doubt on your thinking. Others can often see your jumps in logic better than you can. They can help you challenge the old beliefs that get you into emotional or behavioral trouble.

Furthermore, working with others gives you more support and encouragement for sticking with the hard but rewarding work of challenging your irrational beliefs. At times you will be tempted to quit the fight. Your feelings and behaviors won't seem to be changing fast enough. You will want to give up and return to your old thoughts, which simply keep alive your old feelings and behaviors.

In working with another person or with a group, let me offer the following steps:

Step 1

Each of you identifies a feeling or a behavior that you don't want and wish to change. You share that with the group.

Step 2

The group asks you, "In what circumstances does that feeling or behavior occur and cause you trouble?" You explain the situation.

Step 3

Then the group asks, "What beliefs do you have about that situation that trigger your feeling or behavior?" You, with the help of the group, then identify and write out the beliefs you have that create your response. Don't stop too quickly with the immediate and obvious beliefs. Keep digging for deeper, more foundational beliefs. Here's where the group can help by asking questions to get at the less conscious thoughts that are causing you difficulty.

Step 4

After your irrational, unreasonable beliefs have been identified, the group can help you frame more sensible, reasonable beliefs. These beliefs, then, become the challenges to your old thought systems. The basic question the group can ask you is, "What would you have to think in order to feel or act differently in that situation?" Write down these new beliefs.

Step 5

Next try to identify new *behaviors* you can do that will help you act against your old thoughts, feelings and behaviors. Again, the group can help you identify these challenging behaviors.

You can write them down, select several behaviors to do for the week and tell the group specifically what you're going to do to challenge your old thought patterns. Committing yourself publicly often helps motivate you to carry through on your resolutions.

Step 6

Get together a week later to review how you did. The group can encourage you, support you and challenge you to stay with the process. They can also help you adjust your thinking and can invite you to add or subtract certain thoughts or behaviors. Working together on a weekly basis will help you and the others stay consistent in your efforts to change your thinking in order to change your feelings and your behavior.

Conclusion

The skill of thinking reasonably is not a skill you learn once and then have forever – like typing or bike riding. Reasonable thinking needs regular work. It certainly gets easier the longer you work with this skill. But your mind often seems attracted to unreasonableness and irrationality, much like your body feels drawn at times to ice cream and chocolate bars.

I wish you well in your efforts to think reasonably. Any energy you put into developing this skill will result in increased peace of mind, contentment and a sense of personal well-being. By thinking in new, fresh and reasonable ways, you open the door to a more satisfying and fuller life.

Appendix A

Review of Principles for Thinking Reasonably

1. Your thoughts and beliefs create your feelings and behaviors.
2. You are the cause of your feelings and behaviors. Therefore, you have the power to change them.
3. Your old, automatic thoughts have the most influence on your feelings and behaviors.
4. If you want to change your feelings or behaviors, then learn to *doubt* your beliefs or constructs.
5. Keep an open mind to all information coming your way.
6. Actively challenge old beliefs that cause unwanted feelings and behaviors.
7. Dramatic and demanding thoughts need to be challenged in special ways.
8. Along with challenging and changing your thoughts, you can learn to view your environment selectively.
9. Be patient and work hard to change old beliefs into new beliefs.

Appendix B

Review of Beliefs that Lead to Peace of Mind

1. Descriptive rather than judgmental
2. Unique thoughts rather than comparative
3. Cooperative rather than competitive
4. Informative rather than interpretive
5. Optimistic rather than pessimistic
6. Constructive rather than destructive
7. Flexible rather than demanding
8. Broad rather than narrow
9. Light rather than serious
10. Present rather than future or past